May 2013

UN COMPENSATION

United Nations Should Clarify the Process and Assumptions Underlying Secretariat Professional Salaries

UN COMPENSATION

United Nations Should Clarify the Process and Assumptions Underlying Secretariat Professional Salaries

Highlights of GAO-13-526, a report to congressional requesters

Why GAO Did This Study

Several UN member states have expressed concern that UN employee salaries are increasing, and that they have limited understanding of how the UN determines salaries. ICSC determines salaries for Secretariat professional staff according to the Noblemaire Principle, which states that compensation should be high enough to attract civil servants internationally. In practice, the UN bases salaries for employees on salaries for U.S. civil service employees. The General Assembly has stipulated that salaries should be between 110 and 120 percent of U.S. salaries. The UN and the U.S. government also offer employees benefits and allowances.

GAO was asked to review UN compensation. The report examines (1) how the UN sets salaries for Secretariat professional staff; (2) how the UN compares its employees' salaries with U.S. civil service salaries, including the assumptions underlying its process; and (3) how benefits and allowances provided to UN employees compare with those provided to U.S. civil service employees. GAO analyzed UN and U.S. government documents and interviewed U.S. and UN officials and other stakeholders.

What GAO Recommends

GAO recommends that the U.S. Mission to the UN work with other member states to request that ICSC clarify the assumptions of the margin process and make this information available to member states. The Department of State concurred with this recommendation. ICSC did not agree with our conclusion and noted that its methodology is transparent.

View GAO-13-526. For more information, contact Thomas Melito at (202) 512-9601 or melitot@gao.gov.

What GAO Found

The International Civil Service Commission (ICSC) determines changes to each component of United Nations (UN) Secretariat professional employees' salaries and calculates the difference between UN and U.S. civil service salaries annually. ICSC recommends adjustments to the first component, base salaries, each year to align with changes to U.S. civil service base salaries. For example, ICSC calculated that U.S. civil service base salaries, including the impact of tax changes, increased 1.37 percent on January 1, 2010 and recommended that the UN base salary scale increase 1.37 percent on January 1, 2011. To set post adjustments, an additional salary component intended to equalize purchasing power, ICSC calculates the cost of living in each duty station. ICSC monitors changes in inflation, exchange rates, and other factors, and updates post adjustments periodically to reflect those changes. ICSC conducts surveys of UN employees and collects data on prices at least once every 5 years to ensure that post adjustments reflect the cost of several categories of expenditures relative to New York City, such as goods and services, housing, and medical insurance. Additionally, ICSC calculates the margin, or percentage difference, between UN and U.S. civil service salaries each year. If this process shows that the margin has fallen below 110 or exceeded 120, ICSC can recommend changes to bring UN salaries within that range.

GAO found that the reported margin between UN and U.S. civil service salaries has increased over the past 10 years, and ICSC's process for calculating this difference and its underlying assumptions lack clarity. ICSC data show that the margin was 116.9 in 2012, up from 109.3 in 2002. GAO found that ICSC has developed a six-step process for comparing salaries using various assumptions about the populations included in their calculation. While GAO found that ICSC makes reasonable assumptions when calculating the margin, GAO analysis showed that making different assumptions changes the results, from as low as 105.2 up to 126.7 for 2012. However, ICSC's presentation of this margin calculation to member states lacks clarity in that it does not adequately describe the process and its underlying assumptions. While ICSC has documented specific steps of the margin calculation, we found that ICSC has generally not documented the process as a whole.

The UN Secretariat provides benefits that are similar to U.S. civil service benefits, as well as allowances that are similar to those provided to U.S. civil service employees serving overseas. The UN offers its staff various benefits, including retirement and health and life insurance benefits, that are similar to those offered to U.S. civil service employees. The UN offers more generous leave benefits to its employees than the U.S. civil service. The UN also provides allowances such as grants for education and rental subsidies to its employees. Eligibility for these allowances depends on each employee's unique circumstances, which makes it difficult to compare UN allowances to U.S. civil service allowances. However, U.S. civil service employees serving overseas are eligible for some similar allowances.

Contents

Abbreviations

CEB	United Nations Chief Executives Board for Coordination
CSRS	Civil Service Retirement System
FERS	Federal Employees Retirement System
GS	General Schedule
ICSC	International Civil Service Commission
OPM	United States Office of Personnel Management
UN	United Nations
TEF	Tax Equalization Fund
TSP	Thrift Savings Plan

GAO U.S. GOVERNMENT ACCOUNTABILITY OFFICE

441 G St. N.W.
Washington, DC 20548

May 29, 2013

Congressional Requesters

Several member states of the United Nations (UN), including the United States, have expressed concern that UN employee salaries are increasing, and several member states are concerned that they have limited understanding of how the UN determines salaries. The UN system includes the General Assembly, the Security Council, the Secretariat, and separately administered funds, programs, and specialized agencies. To reduce competition for employees among these entities, among other reasons, the UN established a common system of salaries, allowances, and benefits. The common system includes the UN Secretariat, its affiliated programs, 13 specialized agencies, and one related entity.

The UN is guided by the Noblemaire Principle in setting salaries for professional staff at the Secretariat, as well as other UN common system organizations. This principle states that compensation should be set high enough to attract civil servants from all member states, including those member states with the highest paid government employees.[1] In practice, since its inception in 1945, the UN has based salaries for its professional employees on salaries for the U.S. national civil service.[2] The United States enacted a salary freeze for U.S. civil service employees in 2010; base salaries and locality pay remained at 2010 levels until December 31, 2012. However, in 2011, Secretariat professional employees in New York received an increase in their cost-of-living adjustment which increased their salaries. In December 2012, the General Assembly decided to temporarily freeze the cost of living portion of UN salaries for employees

---

[1]The Noblemaire Principle, originating in the League of Nations, was formulated by the Noblemaire Committee in its 1921 report.

[2]Professional staff members are recruited internationally and typically perform work that is analytical, evaluative, conceptual, or creative, and requires at least a bachelor's degree. The UN also employs general service staff members who are recruited locally, such as messengers, clerks, typists, secretaries, and administrative support staff.

GAO-13-526 UN Compensation

posted in New York for 6 months, effective from August 1, 2012, to January 31, 2013.[3]

We were asked to review how compensation for UN employees is determined and to compare salaries and benefits for UN Secretariat employees and U.S. civil service employees. In this report, we examine (1) how the UN sets salaries for Secretariat professional staff; (2) how the UN compares its employees' salaries with U.S. civil service salaries, including the assumptions underlying its process; and (3) how benefits and allowances provided to UN employees compare with benefits and allowances provided to U.S. civil servants.[4]

To determine how the UN sets salaries for Secretariat professional staff, we reviewed relevant documents from the UN's International Civil Service Commission (ICSC) and interviewed ICSC officials and officials from the UN Secretariat's budget office. To determine how the UN compares its employees' salaries with U.S. civil service salaries, we analyzed ICSC's annual reports and other documents showing the calculation of the difference between UN employee and U.S. civil service salaries, and replicated some parts of their process using UN and U.S. data. We reviewed relevant documentation and interviewed ICSC officials to assess the reliability of the data and determined that they were sufficiently reliable for the purposes of reviewing ICSC's margin calculation process. We interviewed ICSC, UN, and member-state officials about ICSC's calculation. To compare benefits and allowances provided to UN employees with benefits and allowances provided to U.S. civil servants, we analyzed documents from ICSC and other UN divisions, as well as documents from the U.S. Office of Personnel Management (OPM) and the Department of State (State). We also interviewed UN, OPM, and State officials about employee benefits and allowances. This report focuses on the compensation of UN Secretariat employees at the professional level, although professional employees of other common system organizations generally receive the same or similar salaries and

---

[3]When the 6-month freeze ended on February 1, 2013, UN Secretariat employees in New York received an increase in their cost-of-living adjustment, which resulted in an almost 2-percent increase in their salaries.

[4]We plan to provide more in-depth information about the value of UN and U.S. civil service employee benefits and allowances in a forthcoming report.

benefits. Appendix I includes more details on our scope and methodology.

We conducted this performance audit from August 2012 to May 2013 in accordance with generally accepted government auditing standards. Those standards require that we plan and perform the audit to obtain sufficient, appropriate evidence to provide a reasonable basis for our findings and conclusions based on our audit objectives. We believe that the evidence obtained provides a reasonable basis for our findings and conclusions based on our audit objectives.

Background

About 30 Percent of UN Secretariat Employees Are Professional Employees

As of June 30, 2012, the Secretariat employed 42,887 people, including 12,289 professional-level employees.[5] The UN Secretariat administers the programs and policies established by the other principal organs of the UN, including the General Assembly and the Security Council. The duties of the Secretariat include administering peacekeeping operations, mediating international disputes, surveying economic and social trends and problems, and preparing studies on human rights and sustainable development. The Secretariat is headquartered in New York City and has employees at other locations throughout the world. The Secretariat is primarily funded through assessed contributions from member states to the UN regular budget. More than half of its professional employees work in departments or offices, such as the Department of Economics and Social Affairs and the Department for General Assembly and Conference Management, while the remainder work in field operations, including peacekeeping missions and some special political missions, regional commissions, and tribunals (see fig. 1).

---

[5]United Nations, *Composition of the Secretariat: Staff Demographics,* Report of the Secretary General, A/67/329 (Aug. 2012).

GAO-13-526 UN Compensation

Figure 1: UN Secretariat Employees by Broad Occupational Groups, Including Professional Employees, 2012

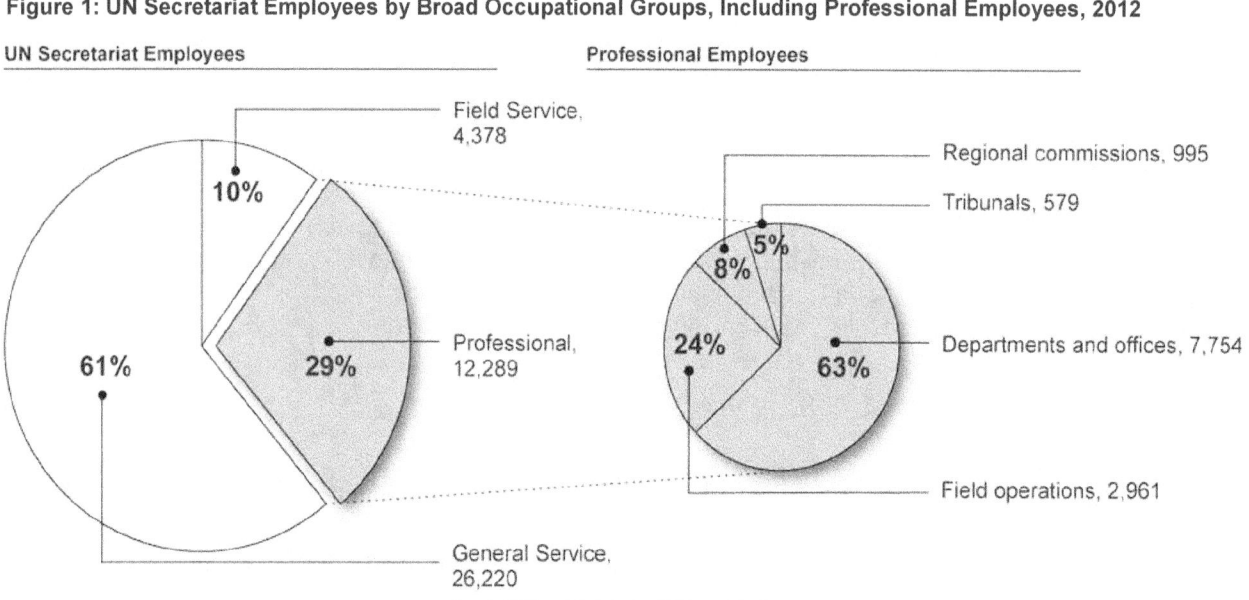

Source: GAO analysis based on UN Secretariat data

| The Noblemaire Principle Guides the UN in Setting Salaries | The UN sets salaries for professional staff according to the Noblemaire Principle, which states that compensation should be set high enough to attract nationals from all member states, including those member states with the highest-paid national civil service employees. Since its inception, the UN has based salaries for professional employees on salaries for the U.S. civil service. The General Assembly passed a resolution in 1985 declaring that average UN net salaries should fall within 110 to 120 percent of average U.S. civil service net salaries, with an average mid-point of 115 over a 5-year period.[6] According to UN officials and documentation, there are three main reasons for setting the margin range higher than U.S. civil service salaries: (1) the relative lack of job stability and security for UN professional staff members compared with U.S. civil servants, (2) the limited promotion potential for UN professional staff members compared with U.S. civil servants, and (3) the fact that a large subset of UN professional staff members are expatriates and therefore |

---

[6]UN General Assembly Resolution A/40/244. For the remainder of this report, we will use the phrase, "the approved margin range," to describe the 110 to 120 percent range and the 5-year average of 115.

incur additional expenses in living away from their home country. The General Assembly has reaffirmed the approved margin range several times since 1985 and as recently as 2011, although representatives from some member states have suggested a lower range may be more appropriate.

ICSC Determines Changes to UN Salaries and Benefits, Subject to General Assembly Approval

The UN General Assembly established ICSC in 1974 as an independent expert body with a mandate to regulate and coordinate the conditions of service of staff in the UN common system. As a part of its mandate, ICSC determines compensation for employees within the UN common system. Each year, ICSC makes recommendations to the General Assembly to change base salaries to align them with any change in U.S. civil service salaries. The General Assembly must approve ICSC's recommendations for the proposed changes to take effect. In addition, ICSC determines the cost-of-living component of UN salaries, called the post adjustment, without prior approval from the General Assembly. ICSC also has the authority to make decisions and take action independently on some routine compensation matters, such as establishing rates for some allowances and benefits. For example, ICSC may set the amount of hardship allowance for a duty station without General Assembly approval.[7]

ICSC is required to submit an annual report to the General Assembly that includes information on the implementation of its decisions and recommendations. In practice, the General Assembly refers ICSC's report and any recommendations to the Fifth Committee, the UN's administrative and budgetary committee. The Fifth Committee considers ICSC's recommendations, including any financial implications of its proposals on the UN budget, and reports its draft resolutions and recommendations to the General Assembly. The General Assembly makes the final decision and issues resolutions on ICSC's recommendations. Member states provide input and vote on ICSC's recommendations through the Fifth Committee and the General Assembly.

---

[7]The UN provides an annual hardship allowance to staff on assignment in duty stations where living and working conditions are difficult.

ICSC Determines Changes to Each Component of UN Salaries, Then Calculates the Difference between UN and U.S. Salaries

ICSC makes recommendations to change UN base salaries to align with changes to U.S. civil service salaries, determines the cost of living at each duty station to set post adjustments, and calculates the difference between UN and U.S. civil service salaries. To set the primary compensation component — base salaries— ICSC analyzes changes in U.S. civil service salaries annually and makes a recommendation to the General Assembly to align the UN base salary scale with U.S. civil service salaries. To set the second compensation component—post adjustment—ICSC monitors changes in the cost of living at each duty station monthly and modifies each post adjustment periodically to account for these changes. This process typically results in changes to UN net salaries, which include base salary and post adjustment, one or more times during the year. Once a year, ICSC calculates the margin, or percentage difference, between average UN net salaries and average U.S. civil service salaries, to determine if average UN net salaries fall within the approved range of 110 to 120 percent of average U.S. civil service salaries. If the result of this calculation shows that UN net salaries fall outside the approved range, ICSC may recommend or make changes to bring average UN net salaries within the approved range.

ICSC Recommends Changes to UN Base Salaries to Align with U.S. Civil Service Base Salaries and Determines a Cost-of-Living Adjustment for Each Post

ICSC Recommends Changes to UN Base Salaries to Align with U.S. Civil Service Base Salaries

ICSC makes a recommendation to change the UN base salary scale each year based on its calculation of changes to salaries for U.S. civil service employees. According to ICSC documents, ICSC follows this process to ensure that UN employees receive at least the base salary of comparable U.S. civil service employees, regardless of duty station. The UN base salary scale also ensures that UN employees around the world at the same grade and step receive at least the same minimum compensation (see fig. 2). ICSC also uses the base salary to calculate post adjustments. The UN salary scale for professional employees includes five professional grades, two director grades, the assistant secretary-general level and the under-secretary-general level. The U.S. General Schedule, the pay system covering the majority of white-collar U.S. civil service employees, includes 15 grades; for comparison purposes, ICSC only considers grades 9 and higher to be professional grades. In addition, the U.S. civil service includes positions above grade 15, called the Senior Executive Service. Each of the UN professional and director grades is divided into 6 to 15 steps and each of the U.S. General Schedule grades is divided into 10 steps. UN and U.S. civil service employees who demonstrate an acceptable level of performance may receive step increases after a set length of time.

Figure 2: UN Professional Salaries Include a Base Salary and Post Adjustment

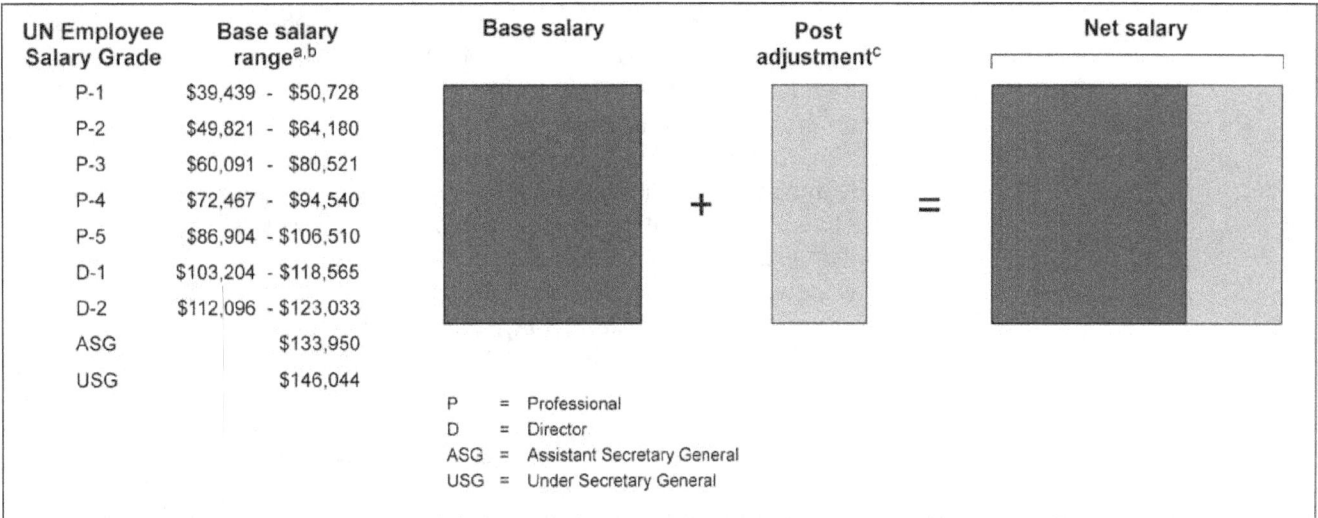

UN Employee Salary Grade	Base salary range[a,b]
P-1	$39,439 - $50,728
P-2	$49,821 - $64,180
P-3	$60,091 - $80,521
P-4	$72,467 - $94,540
P-5	$86,904 - $106,510
D-1	$103,204 - $118,565
D-2	$112,096 - $123,033
ASG	$133,950
USG	$146,044

P = Professional
D = Director
ASG = Assistant Secretary General
USG = Under Secretary General

Source: GAO analysis based on ICSC documents.

Notes:

[a]Base salary ranges in effect as of January 1, 2012.

[b]Base salary ranges shown are for staff members with one or more dependents. Staff members without dependents receive lower base salaries.

[c]Post adjustment amounts vary by duty station.

To determine its recommended adjustment to the UN base salary scale, ICSC calculates the base salary of a U.S. civil service employee at a set point of the U.S. General Schedule and compares it with the base salary for professional employees at an equivalent point of the UN base salary scale. For the purposes of this comparison, ICSC uses the weighted average of the base salaries of U.S. civil servants at grade 13, step 6, and grade 14, step 6, of the U.S. General Schedule as a comparator salary considered to be equivalent to the base salary of a UN employee at the P-4, step 6, grade. ICSC then calculates the percentage increase needed to align the base salary of a UN employee at the P-4, step 6, grade with the comparator salary derived from the U.S. General Schedule.

To assess the extent to which U.S. base salaries have changed each year, ICSC calculates (1) any changes in the comparator salary due to changes published in the U.S. General Schedule, and (2) any changes in tax rates that affect the take-home salary of U.S. civil servants earning the comparator salary who are married and file taxes jointly with their spouse and who have no income other than their U.S. civil service salary. After calculating the change in the comparator salary derived from the U.S. General Schedule, ICSC compares the resulting salary to the base salary of a UN employee at the P-4, step 6, grade who has one or more dependents.[8] The UN pays employees with dependents at a higher rate than those without dependents. According to an ICSC report, this is similar to the practice of many member states that provide a tax advantage for having dependents. Many UN employees are not eligible for these tax advantages, as they might be if they were employed in their national civil service, because most UN employees are not required to pay income taxes on their UN earnings in their home country. However, since some member states may require UN employees to pay taxes on their UN earnings, the UN deducts an amount, called the staff assessment, to determine the base salaries that employees receive. The staff assessment funds are credited to an account, called the Tax Equalization Fund, and are used to reimburse employees who are required to pay income taxes in their home country (see app. II).[9]

After calculating the percentage increase needed to align the P-4, step 6, base salary with the U.S. comparator salary, ICSC makes a recommendation to the General Assembly to increase the UN base salary scale at all grades by the same percentage for the following year. As a result, changes to the UN base salary scale reflect the ICSC-calculated changes in U.S. base salaries for the prior year. In addition, ICSC recommends that the General Assembly decrease post adjustment levels for all duty stations at the same time and by the same amount as the

---

[8]The UN defines a dependent as a spouse with no income or income less than a set threshold, a child under the age of 18, a child between the ages of 18 and 21 who is a full-time student, or a child with a permanent disability, regardless of age.

[9]Currently, the United States is the only member state whose citizens employed by the UN are reimbursed by the TEF.

increase in the base salary scale. As a result, UN net salaries generally do not change when the updated base salary scale goes into effect in any given year, although increases in UN net salaries may occur one or more times during the year through increases in post adjustments. The General Assembly must approve ICSC's recommendations for changes to the base salary scale to take effect. For example, in its 2010 annual report, ICSC recommended a 1.37 percent increase in the UN base salary scale at every grade for 2011 to align UN base salaries with changes in U.S. civil service base salaries, and ICSC also recommended an equivalent decrease in the post adjustment for each duty station. ICSC calculated that the base salary of U.S. civil service employees earning the comparator salary increased 1.37 percent on January 1, 2010, because of an increase in base salaries published in the General Schedule and changes in tax rates. The General Assembly approved the revised salary scale, and it became effective on January 1, 2011.

ICSC Calculates the Post Adjustment at Each Duty Station to Account for Cost of Living Changes

ICSC calculates cost of living, including price differences, inflation, exchange rates, and the average expenditure pattern of staff members, to set a post adjustment for each duty station. ICSC monitors changes in the cost of living at each duty station monthly and updates post adjustments periodically to account for these changes. As a result, UN employees may receive a net salary increase during the year if ICSC's calculation shows that the cost of living in their duty station has increased. In addition, at least once every 5 years, ICSC conducts surveys of UN employees and collects price data to ensure that post adjustments reflect the typical expenditure pattern of UN employees at each location, as well as differences in prices between each duty station and New York City. ICSC has statutory authority to set post adjustments without General Assembly approval. According to ICSC documents and ICSC officials, the UN pays professional employees a post adjustment to ensure that UN employees at each duty station receive a net salary with the same purchasing power as the net salary of UN employees in New York. UN employees in duty stations with a higher cost of living than that of New York receive a higher percentage of their base salary as their post adjustment. As of February 1, 2013, staff members stationed in Romania received the lowest post adjustment, 26 percent of their base salary, and staff members stationed in Japan received the highest post adjustment, 119.7 percent of their base salary. Staff members stationed in New York received a post adjustment equal to 68.7 percent of their base salary.

ICSC monitors changes in exchange rates, inflation, and other factors at each duty station on a monthly basis to calculate the change in cost of living. ICSC also periodically updates the post adjustment for each duty station to account for these changes. As a result, UN employees may receive a net salary increase one or more times throughout the year if ICSC decides to implement a higher post adjustment based on its calculation of the change in cost of living at their duty station. ICSC generally updates post adjustments to account for inflation in duty stations with more stable currencies, called Group I duty stations, less frequently than in duty stations, called Group II duty stations, where currencies may fluctuate rapidly and UN employees may need to spend a larger portion of their income outside the duty station to import goods not available on the local market.[10] In Group I duty stations, such as New York, ICSC typically updates post adjustments every 12 months to account for inflation and other cost increases, although it may change post adjustments earlier if it determines that the cost of living has changed at least 5 percent. For example, UN professional employees in New York received a salary increase in August 2011 when ICSC increased the post adjustment for New York from 61.3 percent of base salary to 65.7 percent of base salary based on its calculation of the increase in the cost of living in New York. In Group II duty stations, ICSC generally reviews post adjustments every 4 months.

ICSC conducts surveys of staff members and collects price data on the cost of goods, services, housing, and other items in each duty station at least once every 5 years. ICSC uses these data to set a new baseline for each duty station's post adjustment. ICSC then follows its procedures described above to monitor changes in the cost of living and update post adjustments as necessary until it conducts a new set of surveys. According to ICSC officials, this process ensures that post adjustments reflect the cost of living for UN employees, who are often living outside their home country and may have different spending patterns than permanent residents of an area. ICSC conducts surveys to estimate the average spending pattern of UN employees. ICSC then calculates the cost of each of five categories of expenditures relative to New York and weights each category based on the spending patterns of UN employees at that duty station:

- *In-area expenditures.* In-area expenditures include goods and services purchased on the local market at the duty station, such as

---

[10]Group I duty stations include those in the United States, Canada, Europe, and Australia, as well as China (Hong Kong), Japan, and French Guiana. ICSC classifies all other duty stations as Group II duty stations.

GAO-13-526 UN Compensation

food and clothing. To set this component, ICSC staff or independent pricing agents collect the prices of over 300 goods and services that are commonly purchased by UN staff at locations popular among UN staff members.

- *Housing.* ICSC calculates this component based on rental prices and the cost of other housing expenses, such as utilities and maintenance.

- *Medical insurance contributions.* ICSC compares data on the amount that staff members pay for medical insurance premiums at each duty station to calculate this component.

- *Pension contributions.* The amount of this component is the same for all duty stations, since all staff members at the same grade and step contribute the same amount to their pensions, regardless of their location.

- *Out-of-area expenditures.* This includes expenditures made outside of a staff member's assigned duty station, such as to purchase items that are not available at the duty station, the cost of private travel outside the duty station, and education costs for dependents living abroad. This component is weighted more heavily in duty stations where staff members may need to import a larger number of items.

ICSC generally follows the same process to calculate the cost of living at all duty stations, although there are some differences between Group I and Group II duty stations. In Group I duty stations, ICSC relies less heavily on survey data and uses more data on prices from sources outside of their own surveys. For example, in Group I duty stations, ICSC uses data from licensed real estate agents to calculate the cost of rent relative to New York, rather than survey data from staff members. In Group II duty stations, ICSC conducts surveys more frequently to account for significant changes in the cost of living due to rapid inflation or devaluation of local currency.

ICSC Calculates Difference between UN Net Salaries and U.S. Civil Service Salaries and May Adjust UN Salaries to Ensure They Fall within Approved Range

The General Assembly requires ICSC to continually review the margin, or percentage difference, between UN and U.S. civil service salaries. ICSC annually calculates the percentage difference between average UN net salaries in New York and average U.S. civil service salaries in Washington, D.C., and submits the results of its calculation to the General Assembly in a report each August. ICSC calculates average UN net salaries in New York using the base salary scale in effect during that year, the post adjustment in effect, and an estimate of any post adjustment increases that are scheduled to take effect later in the year (for a detailed explanation of ICSC's margin calculation process, see the following section). On the basis of the results of this calculation, ICSC may recommend changes to bring UN net salaries within the approved range of 110 to 120 percent of U.S. civil service salaries the following year.

If its annual margin calculation shows that average UN net salaries, including any post adjustment increases scheduled to take effect later in the year, are within the approved range, ICSC implements the post adjustment increases as scheduled. In addition, ICSC recommends an increase in the base salary scale for the following year to align with changes to U.S. civil service salaries, according to its usual process for adjusting the base salary scale. For example, ICSC calculated that, in 2011, average UN net salaries were 114.2 percent of average U.S. civil service salaries, using the UN base salary scale in effect in 2011 and the estimated post adjustment for New York in 2011. Since the margin was within the approved 110 to 120 range, ICSC increased the post adjustment for New York from 61.3 percent of base salary to 65.7 percent of base salary in August 2011, as scheduled. ICSC recalculated the margin once the actual post adjustment increase went into effect and reported a final margin of 114.9 for 2011 in its annual report. ICSC recommended that the General Assembly increase the base salary scale 0.13 percent on January 1, 2012, to align with changes to U.S. civil service salaries. In addition, ICSC recommended that the General Assembly decrease post adjustments for all duty stations by an equivalent amount to ensure that the base salary increase did not provide an additional increase in net salaries.

If the annual margin calculation shows that average UN net salaries have fallen below 110 percent of average U.S. civil service salaries, ICSC makes a recommendation to the General Assembly to increase UN base salaries. According to ICSC officials, the General Assembly has the authority to decide the amount of the increase. The General Assembly may choose to increase the base salary scale to bring the margin up to

110, to the midpoint of 115 that the General Assembly established as a desirable target, or to some other point within the range. For example, in 2002, ICSC determined that the margin was 109.3 and, as a result, recommended an increase in the UN base salary scale, without decreasing the post adjustment, to bring the margin up to 115. The General Assembly approved a smaller increase in the base salary scale than ICSC had recommended which, combined with other changes that affected the margin calculation, increased the margin to 111.9 for 2003.

If ICSC's calculation shows that average UN net salaries would exceed 120 percent of average U.S. civil service salaries, ICSC officials said that they have the authority to act immediately to freeze UN salaries. If ICSC's calculation shows that an estimated increase in the post adjustment in New York scheduled to go into effect later in the year would cause the margin to exceed 120 percent, ICSC officials said that they would not enact the full post adjustment increase. However, officials said that they might enact part of the increase. For example, according to an ICSC report, if granting a scheduled 5-percent increase in post adjustment would increase the margin to 123 percent, ICSC would not grant the full 5-percent cost-of-living increase but might grant a 2-percent increase to keep the margin at or below 120 percent. ICSC officials said that if they were to freeze scheduled post adjustment increases for New York, they would also freeze post adjustments for all other duty stations. In practice, ICSC has not reported a margin above 120 percent since 1986, the first year after the General Assembly decided that UN salaries should remain within a margin of 110 to 120 percent of U.S. civil service salaries.

ICSC's Reported Difference between UN and U.S. Civil Service Salaries Has Increased; ICSC's Process and Related Assumptions for Calculating This Difference Lack Clarity

According to ICSC, the margin between UN and U.S. civil service salaries increased from 109.3 percent in 2002 to 116.9 percent in 2012.[11] We determined that ICSC has a complex process for calculating the margin. The process relies on several assumptions that we found to be reasonable, as they adhere to the General Assembly's intent to compare the salaries of UN professional employees to those of U.S. civil service employees in comparable professional grades. Nevertheless, our analysis shows that using the same process but incorporating alternative reasonable assumptions would yield different results. ICSC has explained some of its assumptions in documents focused on discrete parts of the margin calculation process. However, we found that ICSC does not clearly state all of its assumptions when reporting the margin in its annual reports, and it has not comprehensively explained the process and its assumptions in any single source. This lack of clarity may limit member states' ability to provide oversight of the margin calculation process, consider alternatives, and decide whether the ICSC's recommendations are consistent with the goal of managing the UN budget as effectively as possible.

ICSC's Calculated Margin between UN and U.S. Civil Service Salaries Increased between 2002 and 2012

The results of ICSC's annual calculations show that the margin, or percentage difference, between the average salaries of UN employees in New York and those of U.S. civil service employees in Washington, D.C., increased from 109.3 in 2002 to 116.9 in 2012 (see table 1). As noted above, ICSC calculates the margin each year to compare UN with U.S. salaries and to ensure that any changes to the post adjustment for New York do not result in a margin outside of the approved range of 110 to 120 percent, while generally aiming for a 5-year average of 115 percent. ICSC presents the results of the margin calculation, along with any recommendations for salary adjustments, to the General Assembly in its annual reports. Since the last increase in U.S. civil service base salaries and locality pay in January 2010, ICSC's reported margin has increased from 113.3 in 2010 to 116.9 in 2012, due to changes in the post adjustment for UN employees in New York. According to ICSC officials, they have not recommended that the General Assembly freeze UN salaries because the margin has not exceeded 120. Nevertheless, the

---

[11]ICSC officials told us that they recalculate the margin before the General Assembly makes a decision on pay adjustments, and that, if necessary, they present a revised margin figure, which appears in the General Assembly resolutions. In such cases, we use the revised figure, rather than the original one in the annual report.

General Assembly decided in December 2012 to freeze the implementation of the updated New York post adjustment for 6 months.

Table 1: International Civil Service Commission's Reported Margin between UN and U.S. Salaries, 2002 to 2012

Year	Net salary margin	5-year average
2002	109.3	112.5
2003	110.9	111.7
2004	110.3	111.0
2005	111.1	110.5
2006	114.3	111.2
2007	114.0	112.3
2008	114.7	112.9
2009	113.8	113.6
2010	113.3	114.0
2011	114.9	114.1
2012	116.9	114.9

Source: GAO analysis of ICSC data.

ICSC Uses a Complex, Six-Step Process for Calculating the Margin

Since 1976, ICSC has conducted an annual calculation of the margin between UN and U.S. salaries, using a complex process with six steps, shown in figure 3. The first two steps of the margin calculation are a Noblemaire study, to determine which country has the best-paid civil service, and a grade equivalency study, to match UN and U.S. pay scales. ICSC conducts each of these studies every 5 years, and the results serve as the foundation for ICSC's annual margin calculation. The third, fourth, and fifth steps in the process are to calculate UN net salaries by grade in New York, average U.S. salaries by grade in Washington, D.C., and the margin by grade. In the sixth step, ICSC adjusts these margins by grade for cost of living, to determine the margin between UN and U.S. salaries. See appendix III for a detailed description of each step in ICSC's margin calculation process, along with the assumptions associated with them.

Figure 3: International Civil Service Commission's Net Salary Margin Calculation Process

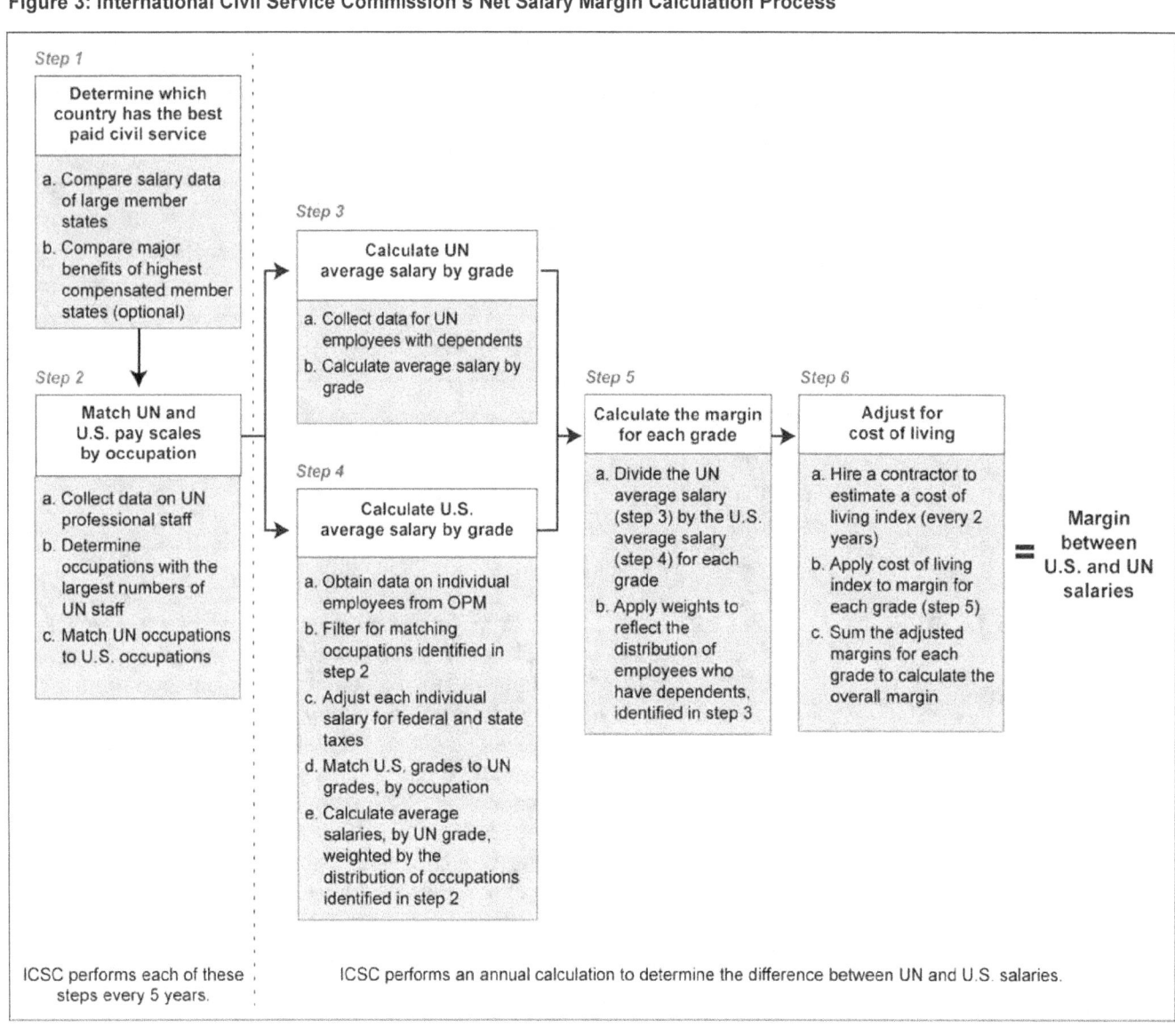

Step 1

Determine which country has the best paid civil service

a. Compare salary data of large member states

b. Compare major benefits of highest compensated member states (optional)

Step 2

Match UN and U.S. pay scales by occupation

a. Collect data on UN professional staff

b. Determine occupations with the largest numbers of UN staff

c. Match UN occupations to U.S. occupations

Step 3

Calculate UN average salary by grade

a. Collect data for UN employees with dependents

b. Calculate average salary by grade

Step 4

Calculate U.S. average salary by grade

a. Obtain data on individual employees from OPM

b. Filter for matching occupations identified in step 2

c. Adjust each individual salary for federal and state taxes

d. Match U.S. grades to UN grades, by occupation

e. Calculate average salaries, by UN grade, weighted by the distribution of occupations identified in step 2

Step 5

Calculate the margin for each grade

a. Divide the UN average salary (step 3) by the U.S. average salary (step 4) for each grade

b. Apply weights to reflect the distribution of employees who have dependents, identified in step 3

Step 6

Adjust for cost of living

a. Hire a contractor to estimate a cost of living index (every 2 years)

b. Apply cost of living index to margin for each grade (step 5)

c. Sum the adjusted margins for each grade to calculate the overall margin

= Margin between U.S. and UN salaries

ICSC performs each of these steps every 5 years.

ICSC performs an annual calculation to determine the difference between UN and U.S. salaries.

Source: GAO analysis based on ICSC documents.

Note: ICSC officials noted that some parts of steps 5 and 6 have been done in a different order, and not as completely separate steps. However, we found that the order of these steps does not change the calculated margin, and describing the steps separately increases the clarity of the process.

ICSC's process for calculating the margin is complex, in part because it is difficult to make a direct comparison between UN and U.S. salaries. To address this challenge, ICSC compares a subset of UN and U.S.

employees that have similar characteristics rather than make a direct comparison of all employees. For example, in the grade equivalency study (step 2 of the process), ICSC limits the comparison to UN staff who are in occupations with a large number of professional staff. More specifically, we determined from ICSC officials and documents that ICSC does the following in performing its grade equivalency study:

a. Collects individual data on UN staff from all UN common system organizations.

b. ICSC analyzes the UN staff data to determine the occupations in the UN common system that have the largest numbers of professional staff. ICSC officials said that they usually include occupations until at least 80 percent of all UN professional staff are represented in their calculation.

c. ICSC matches UN occupations to U.S. occupations. To do so, ICSC purchases data from the Office of Personnel Management (OPM) on U.S. civil service positions in the Washington, D.C., area and analyzes these data to request U.S. agency job descriptions with similar job titles.[12] The UN then analyzes job descriptions for these matches, using OPM's Handbook of Occupational Groups and Families, and applies UN criteria to determine how they would be graded under the UN system. Finally, ICSC creates a grade equivalency matrix with the results, which show how frequently a specific occupation type in a U.S. grade is classified in particular UN grades.

ICSC's Process for Calculating the Margin Relies on a Reasonable Set of Assumptions

ICSC's process for calculating the margin between UN and U.S. civil service salaries relies on several assumptions that define the subset of employees it is comparing. We found these assumptions to be reasonable because they are consistent with the General Assembly's broad goal of comparing the salaries of UN professional staff to those of comparable U.S. civil service employees. Consistent with Generally Accepted Government Auditing Standards, a process has reasonable assumptions if the evidence it produces is sufficient and appropriate to decision making.[13] In order to determine the reasonableness of ICSC's

---

[12]ICSC officials said that they are not always able to obtain data from other agencies that use pay plans other than the GS.

[13]GAO, *Government Auditing Standards, 2011 Revision,* GAO-12-331G (Washington, D.C.: December 2011) and *Designing Evaluations, 2012 Revision,* GAO-12-208G (Washington, D.C.: January 2012).

assumptions, we considered whether the reported margin was consistent with the General Assembly's goal of comparing the salaries of UN professional staff with those of U.S. civil service employees for the purpose of determining whether UN salary levels are consistent with the Noblemaire Principle.

In defining the subset of UN and U.S. civil service employees whose salaries are being compared, ICSC's margin calculation process makes eight assumptions, as shown in table 2. We clarified the reason that ICSC made each assumption with ICSC officials and found that the assumptions were consistent with the General Assembly's goal for this analysis. For example, ICSC assumes that UN employees on the dependency rate are the most appropriate comparison group because UN staff members with dependents account for the majority of UN employees. ICSC officials said that they exclude employees without dependents because most new hires fall into this category, so including these employees in the margin calculation might reflect changes in hiring patterns rather than changes in actual salary levels. According to ICSC officials, excluding employees without dependents leads to a more stable and consistent margin value over time and prevents the need for corrections in the margin calculation.

Table 2: Assumptions the International Civil Service Commission Makes in Calculating the Margin between UN and U.S. Civil Service Salaries

Steps	Assumption	Impact on margin calculation process
1	Per capita income is representative of civil service salaries in a country.	Potentially leads to exclusion of countries with civil service salaries that are outliers relative to their country's average, but provides a simple way to narrow the list of comparators
1, 2, 3, 4, 5, 6	Employees in headquarters locations are representative of all employees.	Potentially excludes employees in locations that are outliers relative to headquarters, but reduces time and staff needed for step 6 while focusing on areas with the most employees.
2, 3, 4, 5	Employees receiving the dependency rate are representative of UN salary of all professional staff.	Excludes employees without dependents, who are paid lower salaries and who are more likely to be distributed at the lower UN grades, but prevents shocks in the annual margin calculation due to the greater stability of dependency rate employees.
2, 3, 4, 5	Occupations with the most staff are representative of all UN occupations.	Excludes employees in occupations with fewer staff who may be paid differently than those in more common occupations, but increases the likelihood that there are sufficient data to draw a comparison between UN and U.S. civil service employees.
3, 4, 5	The proportion of staff in each occupation is relatively stable for a 5-year period.	Includes occupations in the annual margin calculation that may have shrunk and excludes those that may have grown since the most recent grade equivalency study, but reduces the cost of conducting more frequent grade equivalency studies.
4, 5	All U.S. civil service employees are married and file jointly.	Decreases the accuracy of U.S. average net salary calculations, but enables ICSC to make a comparison despite limited data and uses the U.S. filing status that is most comparable to the UN dependency rate.
4, 5	U.S. civil service employees use the average deductions in their state.	Decreases the accuracy of U.S. average net salary calculations, but enables ICSC to make a comparison despite limited data on U.S. civil service employees' state income taxes.
6	Differences in salary between two locations are associated with the cost of living in those locations.	Margin comparison considers the purchasing power of employees rather than the cost of labor for those employees as in U.S. locality pay differentials, but the former is consistent with the UN's post adjustment.

Legend: Step 1 = Determine which country has the best paid civil service; Step 2 = Match UN and U.S. pay scales, by occupation; Step 3 = Calculate UN average salary by grade; Step 4 = Calculate U.S. average salary by grade; Step 5 = Calculate the margin for each grade; Step 6 = Adjust for cost of living.

Source: GAO analysis of ICSC source documents and interviews.

In addition, ICSC limits its comparison to UN employees in New York City and U.S. civil service employees in Washington, D.C. ICSC acknowledges that some of the difference in salaries between the two groups is due to the difference in their locations, and uses a cost-of-living adjustment to correct for this difference. This adjustment assumes that the differences in salary reflect differences in purchasing power in New York City versus Washington, D.C. The margin calculation adjusts for the differences in costs for some expenses common to both locations, including housing, transportation, and food. ICSC hires an independent organization to estimate the total cost-of-living difference between the two locations. This adjustment is commonly used in economics to control for such cost differences, and it allows for a more accurate comparison of UN and U.S. employees' salaries than if no adjustment had been made.

Alternative Margin Calculation Assumptions Would Also Achieve the General Assembly's Goal but Change the Results

While we found that the ICSC makes reasonable assumptions when calculating the margin, we found that making different assumptions, which are also reasonable, changes the results. Our analysis of some potential alternatives produced a range of different margins that vary from 105.2 to 126.7. Specifically, we recalculated the 2012 margin by changing one or more of ICSC's assumptions, resulting in five alternative scenarios (see table 3).[14] The first assumption we modified was ICSC's assumption that employees receiving the dependency rate are representative of the average net UN salary of all professional staff. To examine the impact of this assumption on the final margin result, we calculated the margin in a scenario where only employees without dependents are included, and another scenario where employees receiving both the dependency and the single rates are included. Changing these assumptions resulted in changes in two inputs to ICSC's calculation: average UN salary[15] and the distribution of staff among UN professional grades. Including only employees without dependents, who receive a lower salary, resulted in a lower margin of 105.2, while including both those employees and employees with dependents resulted in a margin of 108.0.[16]

---

[14] We did not comprehensively analyze all of the alternative assumptions that could be made in ICSC's process, but rather analyzed an illustrative few for which we were able to obtain relevant data. Because the most appropriate alternative is dependent on the need for information to make decisions, and because member states and the General Assembly are ultimately the users of this information, we are not endorsing any of these alternatives as the most appropriate.

[15] Because we did not have data on actual UN salaries, we used the base salary with the New York post adjustment at step 4 of each grade in these calculations. The results would likely be different if actual salary data were used.

[16] One limitation of these two results, however, is that we did not have ICSC data on U.S. tax liabilities, and thus the comparison group was still U.S. civil service employees who were assumed to be married and filing jointly. Ideally, we would consider only those U.S. employees whose filing status is single for the first comparison, and all U.S. employees in the second comparison.

Table 3: 2012 Margin Results under Selected Alternative Scenarios

Scenario[a]	New margin result[b]
ICSC reported margin for 2012	117.7
1. Assume that employees without dependents are representative of all UN staff (only include them in the calculation)c	105.2
2. Do not assume a specific salary rate distribution for UN employees (include both dependency-rate and single-rate UN employees)	108.0
3. Assume that cost of labor explains the difference in salary in the two locations (use cost of labor instead of cost of living)	126.7
4. Assumptions 1 and 3 above: only include UN employees without dependents and use cost of labor	113.3
5. Assumptions 2 and 3 above: include both dependent-rate and single-rate UN employees, and use cost of labor	116.3[c]

Source: GAO analysis of ICSC data.

Notes:

[a]Because relevant data were not available, we did not analyze scenarios in which a different subset of occupations, or all occupations, were included, nor did we analyze scenarios with alternative assumptions about the tax liabilities of U.S. civil service employees. Such scenarios would I kely have different results from those included.

[b]In scenarios 1, 2, 4, and 5, the comparison group is U.S. civil service employees who are married and filing jointly. These results would be different if only single U.S. employees, or both single and U.S. employees with dependents, were included, as they would be in an ideal comparison. However, we did not analyze these scenarios because we did not have ICSC data on U.S. tax liabilities.

[c]Because relevant data on UN salaries were not available, we used step 4 of the base salary with the New York post adjustment in scenarios 1,2,4 and 5.

The next assumption we modified was the assumption that differences in salary between two locations are associated with the cost of living in those locations. To examine the impact of this assumption on the final margin result, we calculated the margin using the cost of labor, as used by the federal government in setting U.S. civil service locality pay. The UN uses the cost of living in the margin calculation process to estimate the purchasing power of UN employees' salaries. The cost of labor that we used in our alternative scenario represents an estimate of the market wage for a U.S. government position.[17] Using a cost-of-labor measure, we calculated a higher margin of 126.7.

---

[17]In calculating its own locality pay among different regions, OPM uses the cost of labor.

We also modified both of these previous assumptions, resulting in two additional scenarios. The first includes only employees without dependents and uses the cost of labor to adjust for differences between New York and Washington, D.C. The second scenario includes both employees with dependents and those without dependents, and also uses the cost of labor. Overall, the change from using the cost of living to using the cost of labor led to the highest calculated margin result, and including only employees without dependents led to the lowest calculated margin result.

ICSC's Presentation of the Margin Calculation Process and Underlying Assumptions Are Unclear

ICSC has not adequately described its margin calculation process, or its underlying assumptions, in its annual reports to the General Assembly or other documents. The *Standards for Internal Controls in the Federal Government* states that information should be recorded and communicated to management and others within the entity who need it and in a form and within a time frame that enables them to carry out their internal control and other responsibilities.[18] We reviewed ICSC annual reports, as well as various internal reports and summary documents that ICSC provided us, and found that none of these documents comprehensively described the ICSC margin calculation process and its underlying assumptions. For example, when adjusting U.S. average salaries for tax liabilities, ICSC assumes that all U.S. civil service employees are married and filing their taxes jointly with their spouse, even though some of these employees may file as single or as married but filing separately from their spouse. However, ICSC does not note in its annual report that this assumption does not precisely reflect the population of U.S. civil service employees included in the calculation, and therefore member states are not given adequate information to understand how ICSC has defined this population. ICSC officials told us that the data available to ICSC do not indicate actual filing status or tax liability for U.S. civil service employees and that the assumed filing status of married filing jointly and with dependents is the most comparable to employees receiving the dependency rate in the UN, thus allowing for a better comparison of the two populations. As noted above, the assumptions underlying the margin calculation process directly affect how

---

[18]GAO, Standards for Internal Control in the Federal Government (supersedes AIMD-98-21.3.1), AIMD-00-21.3.1 (Washington, D.C.: November 1999). We are suggesting this as a best practice.

the populations are being compared, and different assumptions yield different results.

Additionally, ICSC has not provided a comprehensive explanation to member states about its process. Representatives from four UN member states, including representatives from the U.S. Mission to the UN in New York, said that they did not understand the entire margin calculation process and that ICSC's attempts to explain the process had not improved their understanding of it. Although officials from ICSC provided us with a range of historical and summary documents about parts of their process, no single document comprehensively described the entire margin calculation process, including its underlying assumptions. While ICSC has documented aspects of specific steps of the margin calculation, we found that ICSC has generally not documented the process as a whole.

UN Benefits Are Generally Similar to Those Offered to U.S. Civil Service Employees, and UN Allowances Are Similar to Allowances for U.S. Civil Service Employees Serving Overseas

The UN Secretariat provides numerous benefits that are similar to U.S. civil service benefits, and UN employees receive a number of allowances that are similar to those available to U.S. civil service employees serving overseas. The UN offers its staff various benefits, including retirement, health insurance, and life insurance benefits, that are similar to benefits offered to U.S. civil service employees. The UN also provides allowances, such as education grants and rental subsidies, to its employees. Eligibility for these allowances depends on each employee's unique circumstances, which makes it difficult to compare UN allowances to U.S. civil service allowances. However, UN employees are eligible for a similar array of allowances as U.S. civil service staff serving outside of the United States.

UN Retirement and Insurance Benefits Are Similar to U.S. Civil Service Benefits, but UN Secretariat Employees Accrue More Leave than U.S. Employees

Retirement benefits

Retirement benefits for both UN and U.S. employees are administered through separate agencies. UN retirement benefits are administered by the UN Joint Staff Pension Fund, which was established in 1949 to provide retirement, survivor, and disability benefits for UN staff. U.S. civil service retirement benefits are administered by OPM, under two systems: the Civil Service Retirement System (CSRS), and the Federal Employees Retirement System (FERS), which generally covers employees first hired in 1984 or later. According to a UN official, the UN retirement benefits package is structured to be comparable to CSRS.

The UN and U.S. retirement systems share some similarities in terms of retirement age, contribution amounts, and the amount of the retirement benefit. The age at which UN employees generally qualify for retirement benefits is 60 for employees who began working at the UN before January 1, 1990, and 62 for employees who began after January 1, 1990. For U.S. civil servants under CSRS and FERS, employees can retire at 60 with at least 20 years of service or 62 with at least 5 years of service, though a person with 30 years or more of service may retire earlier. UN employees contribute 7.9 percent of their salary to their retirement plan, and CSRS employees contribute 7, 7.5, or 8 percent, depending on their position.[19] FERS employees contribute a much lower amount of their salary to their retirement plan, 0.8 percent, and receive a smaller annual retirement, but also have the option of contributing to a defined contribution plan with a federal matching component, called the Thrift Savings Plan (TSP). As of January 1, 2013, newly hired employees covered by FERS contribute 3.1 percent and the employer contributes 9.6

---

[19]Regular federal employees contribute 7 percent of their basic pay to their pensions under CSRS. Law enforcement officers, firefighters, and congressional employees pay 7.5 percent. Members of Congress, bankruptcy judges, judges of the U.S. Court of Military Appeals, and employees of the United States Magistrate contribute 8 percent.

percent. FERS employees also pay an additional 6.2 percent of their salary (up to $113,700) in Social Security taxes. In 2013, federal employees could contribute a maximum of $17,500 to their TSP. Appendix IV contains detailed information about UN and U.S. civil service retirement plans.

The value of the retirement benefit for UN and U.S. civil service employees differs from employee to employee, depending on their years of service, their highest salary, and, for U.S. civil service staff under the FERS plan, the amount that they contributed to their TSP. For example, for a UN employee who retired at age 65 with 20 years of service and a final average remuneration of $100,000, the annual retirement benefit would be $36,250.[20] An equivalent U.S. civil service employee who retired at age 65 with 20 years of service and an average final salary of $100,000 would also have an annual retirement benefit of $36,250 under the CSRS system. An equivalent U.S. civil service employee under the FERS system would have an annual retirement benefit of $22,000 plus any additional income earned from his or her TSP, depending on his or her contributions and investment choices.

In 2011, ICSC published a study comparing UN and U.S. retirement plans, and concluded that UN and U.S. FERS employee income replacement rates, the percentage of pre-retirement income replaced by retirement income, are comparable if employee contributions are similar.[21] The study found that the income replacement rate for UN retirees was 55.6 percent, meaning that UN employees can expect to replace 55.6 percent of their salaries after they retire. According to the study, U.S. employees can expect to replace 54.7 percent of their salaries after retirement if they contribute 0.9 percent of their salaries to TSP, or 78.4 percent if they contribute 9.4 percent of their salaries to TSP.

---

[20]The UN defines final average remuneration as the annual average pensionable remuneration within the 36 completed calendar months of highest pensionable remuneration within the last 5 years of service. OPM defines the average high-three salary for CSRS and FERS employees as the largest annual rate resulting from averaging an employee's basic pay in effect over any period of 3 consecutive years of service, with each rate weighted by the length of time it was in effect.

[21]United Nations, *Comparison of the United States/United Nations Income Replacement Ratios*, ICSC/72/R.4 (2011).

Health Benefits and Life Insurance	Both UN and U.S. civil service employees are eligible for health insurance and life insurance. UN Secretariat employees working in headquarters have a choice of several preferred provider organization plans, and the amount they pay for their insurance depends on whether their insurance also covers their spouse and children. UN Secretariat employees working outside of the United States are covered by a self-funded health benefit plan that reimburses employees for medical expenses around the world. For UN Secretariat employees working at the UN headquarters in New York City, the UN covers 33 percent of the cost of the health insurance premium, and for employees working outside of the United States, the UN covers 50 percent. The monthly cost of UN employee health insurance premiums in 2012 ranged from $610 to $2,286, depending on the plan chosen and whether dependents were insured. The amount that UN employees contributed ranged from 3.4 percent of their salary to 9.7 percent of their salary, depending on the plan and whether dependents are insured. U.S. civil service employees are eligible for a much wider array of health insurance plans, which vary from state to state, and also range in cost depending on whether the insurance covered the employee's spouse and children. Employee premiums for nationwide plans in 2012 ranged from $93 to $638 per month, depending on the plans and whether it covered dependents. U.S. civil service employees working outside of the United States are also generally eligible for health insurance.

The UN Secretariat offers its employees the option of enrolling in a group life insurance plan, but covers none of the cost of the insurance. U.S. civil service employees are automatically enrolled in a group life insurance plan, unless they waive the coverage. The U.S. government covers one-third of the cost of this insurance and two-thirds is covered by the employee.

Leave Benefits

While both organizations offer leave benefits, UN Secretariat employees are eligible for more generous leave benefits than U.S. civil service employees. For example, UN employees earn more annual leave than U.S. civil service employees. UN employees on fixed terms contracts earn 30 days of annual leave a year, while U.S. civil service employees earn 26 days a year once they have 15 or more years of service. U.S. civil service employees with fewer than 3 years of service earn 13 days of annual leave a year, and those with 3 but less than 15 years of service earn 20 days per year. In addition, UN employees can be eligible for more sick leave than U.S. civil service employees, depending on length of service. UN employees do not earn sick leave the way they earn annual leave. Those with a need for sick leave who have worked for the UN for fewer than 3 years are entitled to sick leave of up to 3 months on full salary and 3 months on half salary. UN employees who have completed 3 or more years of service are entitled to up to 9 months of sick leave. In contrast, U.S. civil service employees earn 4 hours of sick leave per pay period, or 1 day per month, and may carry over unlimited amounts of sick leave into subsequent years. In addition, UN employees are entitled to paid maternity and paternity leave as well as paid leave to adopt a child, which is not offered to U.S. civil service employees; they are entitled to take certain amounts of time away from work for these purposes, but must use either their paid leave or unpaid leave under the Family and Medical Leave Act to account for their absences. Both UN and U.S. employees have 10 holidays per year, though this number may vary for UN employees depending on their duty station. U.S. civil service employees have some types of paid leave not available to UN Secretariat employees, including leave to serve as a juror or a witness, leave for bone marrow and organ donation, limited amounts of leave for certain types of military service, and leave sharing programs which allow employees to donate annual leave to colleagues who have certain emergency needs. Table 4 compares leave benefits for UN and U.S. civil service employees.

Table 4: Comparison of Leave Benefits for UN Secretariat and U.S. Civil Service Employees

	UN employees	U.S. Civil Service employees
Annual leave	UN employees on fixed-term contracts accrue 2.5 working days per month (30 days per year), and may carry over up to 60 days per year.	Full-time employees with fewer than 3 years of service earn 4 hours annual leave per bi-weekly pay period (13 days per year.) Those with 3 but less than 15 years of service earn 6 hours of annual leave per bi-weekly pay period and 10 hours of annual in the last pay period of the year (20 days per year.) Those with 15 or more years of service earn 8 hours per bi-weekly pay period (26 days per year). Senior Executive Service, Senior Level, Scientific or Professional employees and employees in equivalent pay systems earn 8 hours of leave per bi-weekly pay period, regardless of years of service. At its discretion, an agency may advance annual leave to an employee in an amount not to exceed the amount the employee would accrue within the year. Employees stationed in the United States may carry over 30 days of annual leave. Those stationed overseas may carry over 45 days, and Senior Executive Service employees may carry over 90 days.

	UN employees	U.S. Civil Service employees
Sick leave	Employees with fewer than 3 years of service are entitled to up to 3 months of full salary and 3 months on half salary, of certified sick leave. Employees with more than 3 years of service are entitled to up to 9 months of full salary and 9 months of half salary of certified sick leave. Employees are also entitled to up to 7 days of uncertified sick leave, which can be used for purposes such as family emergencies. UN employee sick leave does not accumulate.	Full-time employees accrue 4 hours of sick leave for each bi-weekly pay period (13 days per year.) There is no limitation on the amount of sick leave that can be accumulated. There is no limitation on how much sick leave an employee may use for his or her own personal medical needs. A full-time employee may only use up to 13 days of sick leave for general family care and bereavement purposes and up to 12 weeks of sick leave to care for a family member with a serious health condition each year. An employee is entitled to no more than a combined total of 12 weeks of sick leave each year for all family care purposes. At its discretion, an agency may advance up to 13 or 30 days of sick leave (depending on the reason for which sick leave is advanced) to an employee, when required by the exigencies of the situation, for the same reasons it grants sick leave to an employee. .
Maternity leave	Leave with full pay for a total period of 16 weeks (usually 6 weeks prior to anticipated date of delivery and 10 weeks after birth.) Annual leave accrues during maternity leave if employee returns to work after a maximum of 6 months.	The Family and Medical Leave Act of 1993 allows a birth mother to use up to 12 weeks of unpaid leave after childbirth. A birth mother may also use accrued sick leave and annual leave for pregnancy and childbirth.
Paternity leave	Employees are entitled to leave with pay for up to 4 weeks (up to 8 weeks within the 12 months following the child's birth).	The Family and Medical Leave Act of 1993 allows a birth father to use up to 12 weeks of unpaid leave after childbirth. A birth father may also use up to 12 weeks of sick leave and accrued annual leave to care for the mother during pregnancy and childbirth.
Adoption leave	Employees are entitled to special leave with full pay for the adoption of a child.	The Family and Medical Leave Act of 1993 allows parents to use up to 12 weeks of unpaid leave to adopt a child. Parents may also use accrued sick and annual leave for purposes related to the adoption of a child.
Special leave	Employees are entitled to full, partial, or no pay for advanced study or research in the interest of the organization.	
Official holidays	10 holidays per year.	10 federal holidays per year. In addition, federal employees located in Washington, D.C., may receive a federal holiday on Inauguration Day, which occurs every 4 years.

Source: GAO analysis of UN and Office of Personnel Management data.

UN Allowances Are Similar to Allowances for U.S. Civil Service Employees Serving Overseas

UN employee allowances are generally similar to the allowances that are offered to U.S. civil service employees serving overseas.[22] The UN offers numerous allowances, such as education and travel benefits, some of which are intended to compensate their staff for extra expenses that they may incur if they are moving to another country to work for the UN. The rules of eligibility for these allowances vary, so a UN employee's eligibility for an allowance depends on their individual circumstances. U.S. civil service employees working outside of the United States are eligible for some similar allowances. It is difficult to compare UN Secretariat allowances with U.S. civil service allowances because the allowances can vary widely across employees, depending on where they are located, their salary level, and whether they have dependents.

Rental Subsidy

One example of an allowance that the UN offers to its employees is rental subsidies. UN employees who are newly appointed or reassigned are eligible for this entitlement, which is paid to staff members who are generally paying higher rent than what the UN considers to be an average cost for their duty station. Newly hired employees or employees assigned to another duty station are eligible for the rental subsidy for 7 years, and the subsidy declines over time. UN officials explained that the UN's rationale for offering this rental subsidy is that over time, an employee should adjust to their new duty station and find more economical accommodations than they might when they first arrive. For example, an employee who earns a monthly salary of $6,687 might qualify for a maximum rental subsidy of $866 a month if the employee's rent is $2,164 but the UN has determined that the reasonable maximum monthly level is $1070.

Education Grant

UN employees who are serving outside their home country are also eligible for education grants to cover part of the cost of educating their children. This allowance covers 75 percent of costs for children up to age 25 and up to the fourth year of postsecondary education. The maximum that the UN will pay varies by country. As of August 2012, the proposed maximum education grant for employees working in the United States was $32,255. In addition, the UN pays 100 percent of boarding costs for employees posted at some locations where educational facilities are inadequate, in addition to the education grant, up to a maximum amount.

---

[22]For a list of UN employee allowances and comparable allowances for U.S. civil service employees posted overseas, please see Appendix V.

The UN also provides travel expenses for the child for one return journey each year between the school and the duty station, if they are in different countries. If employees are reassigned to their home country after having been eligible for an education grant, they may, to ease the transition, continue to receive the grant for the balance of the school year.

Other Allowances

Other allowances that the UN offers to its employees include dependency, hardship, and mobility allowances, as described below:

- *Children's allowance.* The UN offers an annual, flat-rate children's allowance to all eligible staff. As of August 2012, the amount was $2,929 per child under age 18, or under age 21 if the child was a full-time student. Professional staff with children who do not have a dependent spouse are not eligible for the children's allowance for their first child because they are paid at the dependent rate, though they would receive the allowance for other eligible children.

- *Mobility allowance.* The UN provides a mobility allowance to staff on an assignment of 1 year or more who have had 5 consecutive years of service in the UN system. As of January 2012, the mobility allowance ranged from $2,020 to $16,900. Employees qualify for the mobility allowance if they have accrued 5 consecutive years of service in the UN system. The amount an employee receives varies by the number of assignments, the duty station category whether the employee has dependents, and the employee's salary grade.

- *Hardship allowance.* The UN provides a hardship allowance to staff on assignment in duty stations where living and working conditions are difficult. The hardship allowance varies by position level and dependency status. The allowance varies depending on the employee's duty station, salary level, and whether the employee has dependents. As of August 2012, the allowance ranged from $4,360 to $22,680.

Most of the U.S. allowances that are similar to UN allowances apply only to a small percentage of U.S. civil service employees, specifically those serving overseas. As of December 2012, according to OPM data, approximately 2 percent of US federal civil service employees in professional and administrative occupations were working in other countries.[23] These U.S. civil service employees serving overseas are eligible for housing allowances, relocation expenses, education allowances, and hazard pay, among others.

Conclusions

Since the UN was founded in 1945, it has used U.S. civil service salaries as the basis for establishing its own salaries in an effort to attract civil servants from all over the world, including from the countries that pay the highest civil service salaries. The UN compensation package includes a base salary and a cost-of-living adjustment designed to enable UN employees to adhere to the same standard of living no matter where in the world they are posted. The package also includes retirement benefits, health insurance, and allowances that compensate staff for living overseas. UN salaries have risen compared with U.S. civil service salaries since 2002, but ICSC's annual margin calculation has helped the UN to ensure that the difference between its salaries and U.S. civil service salaries has generally remained within the approved range of 110 and 120 percent. Although we determined that ICSC's margin calculation relies on a reasonable set of assumptions, we also found that reasonable alternative scenarios would change the results. However, without an adequate description of ICSC's current process and the underlying assumptions, member states cannot effectively evaluate whether ICSC's process represents the most appropriate method of comparing the two populations, or determine if another approach would address the General Assembly resolution. Since ICSC uses the margin as the primary basis for making recommendations to adjust UN salaries, member states need this information to adequately consider ICSC's recommendations before deciding whether to accept or reject them.

Recommendation for Executive Action

To enable member states to effectively oversee ICSC's process for setting and adjusting salaries and ensure that its work is in line with General Assembly decisions, the Secretary of State should direct the U.S. Mission to the UN to work with other member states to request that ICSC clarify its process and the underlying assumptions for comparing UN and U.S. salaries and make this information available to member states.

---

[23]These data are from OPM's Enterprise Human Resources Integration data warehouse, which is made available through OPM's FedScope program. The data exclude certain agencies in the Executive branch and the Legislative branch, and all Judiciary branch agencies.

Agency Comments and Our Evaluation

We provided a draft of this report for comment to the Secretary of State; the U.S. Ambassador to the United Nations, who transmitted the draft to ICSC; and the Acting Director of OPM. OPM and ICSC provided us with technical comments, which we incorporated into the report as appropriate. State and ICSC also provided written comments, which are reprinted in appendices VI and VII.

State agreed with our recommendation and noted that it believes that our report provides timely and useful information that will support its efforts to make sure that UN compensation can attract and retain talented staff while ensuring fiscal discipline at the UN. State responded that it would have been useful for the report to express an opinion about which of the alternative assumptions would be optimal for ICSC; to examine the justification for the margin range of 110 to 120 percent; and to quantify the value of UN and U.S. benefits and allowances. We provided information about ICSC's process so that member states may have a better understanding of how ICSC calculates the margin. We did not comment on the justification for setting the margin range at 110 to 120 percent of U.S. civil service salaries, because that was outside the scope of our review. We plan to provide more in-depth information on the value of the allowances and benefits for both UN professional staff and U.S. civil service employees in a forthcoming report.

ICSC's letter expressed concern about our use of the cost-of-labor factor as one of the alternative margin calculation scenarios, noting that the cost-of-living factor that it uses in the margin calculation is also used in the post adjustment system. ICSC also pointed out that our reference to our *Standards for Internal Controls in the Federal Government* as criteria for information standards does not apply to ICSC, and that they are confident that their methodology is transparent and has been fully described and explained. With regard to our use of the cost-of-labor factor, we noted that since UN's remuneration system is based on the Noblemaire Principle, and accordingly UN salaries are based on U.S. civil service salaries, it is reasonable to consider using the same calculation that the U.S. government uses in setting its own locality pay. We also noted that when we changed this assumption in an alternative scenario, it resulted in a calculation of the margin that was above the 110 to 120 range. With regard to ICSC's transparency in reporting, we also noted that we were not able to fully describe the margin process until after extensive document review, use of supplemental data, and several interviews with ICSC officials. Finally, with regard to our use of our own criteria for clarity of information, while we acknowledge that these standards do not apply to ICSC, we note that this is a best practice and that without such information, member states cannot effectively assess whether ICSC's process best satisfies the General Assembly resolution.

We are sending copies of this report to the appropriate congressional members, the Secretary of State, the U.S. Ambassador to the United Nations, the OPM Acting Director and other interested parties. In addition, the report is available at no charge on the GAO Website at http://www.gao.gov.

If you or your staff have any questions about this report, please contact me at (202) 512-9601 or melitot@gao.gov. Contact points for our Offices of Congressional Relations and Public Affairs may be found on the last page of this report. GAO staff who made key contributions to this report are listed in appendix VIII.

Thomas Melito
Director, International Affairs and Trade

List of Requesters

The Honorable Bob Corker
Ranking Member
Committee on Foreign Relations
United States Senate

The Honorable Lindsey Graham
Ranking Member
Subcommittee on State, Foreign Operations, and Related Programs
Committee on Appropriations
United States Senate

The Honorable John Barrasso
United States Senate

The Honorable Richard Burr
United States Senate

The Honorable Tom Coburn
United States Senate

The Honorable James Inhofe
United States Senate

The Honorable Johnny Isakson
United States Senate

The Honorable Mike Lee
United States Senate

The Honorable James Risch
United States Senate

The Honorable Marco Rubio
United States Senate

Appendix I: Objectives, Scope, and Methodology

This report examines (1) how the United Nations (UN) sets salaries for Secretariat professional staff; (2) how the UN compares its employees' salaries with U.S. civil service salaries, including the assumptions underlying its process; and (3) how benefits and allowances provided to UN employees compare with benefits and allowances provided to U.S. civil service employees.

To examine how the UN sets salaries for Secretariat professional staff, we reviewed relevant documents and data from the UN, including International Civil Service Commission (ICSC) annual reports and other documents, and General Assembly resolutions. We conducted interviews in New York City, New York, with several UN offices, including ICSC, and the Office of Program Planning, Budget and Accounts. We met with officials from ICSC's Salaries and Allowances Division to obtain additional information on the UN's process for setting base salaries and met with ICSC's Cost of Living Division to obtain additional information on ICSC's process for establishing post adjustments.

To examine how the UN compares its employees' salaries with U.S. civil service salaries, including the assumptions underlying its process, we analyzed ICSC's annual reports showing their calculation of the difference between UN employee and U.S. civil service salaries. We replicated some parts of their process by supplementing the data in ICSC's 2012 annual report with data received from ICSC and from published UN and U.S. salary scales and locality adjustments. We gathered data from ICSC and the UN Chief Executives' Board for Coordination (CEB) documents to replicate ICSC's margin calculation. We reviewed relevant documentation and interviewed ICSC officials, and determined these data were sufficiently reliable for the purposes of presenting the reported margin result from 2002 to 2012, and analyzing how alternative assumptions would affect the margin result. To obtain additional information on ICSC's process for calculating the difference between UN and U.S. civil service salaries, we met with officials from ICSC and CEB. We reviewed relevant documents, including documents on ICSC's grade equivalency study, margin calculation process, and the cost of living study used in the margin calculation. To supplement this information, we met with officials from the U.S. Mission to the UN in New York and three other member states to obtain their views on ICSC's process for comparing UN and U.S. civil service salaries.

To examine how benefits and allowances provided to UN employees compare with benefits and allowances provided to U.S. civil service employees, we analyzed documents from ICSC and other UN

organizational units, as well as documents from the U.S. Office of
Personnel Management (OPM) and the Department of State. To obtain
additional information on the benefits and allowances provided to
professional staff of the Secretariat, we interviewed officials from the UN's
Office of Human Resources Management. We interviewed officials from
the UN Joint Staff Pension Fund to obtain additional information on
retirement benefits for UN staff members and met with officials from the
Insurance Division of the UN's Office of Human Resources Management
to obtain additional information on health insurance plans available to UN
staff members. We conducted interviews with U.S. government officials in
Washington, D.C., including officials from OPM and State, to obtain
additional information on benefits and allowances offered to U.S. civil
servants.

We conducted this performance audit from August 2012 to May 2013 in
accordance with generally accepted government auditing standards.
Those standards require that we plan and perform the audit to obtain
sufficient, appropriate evidence to provide a reasonable basis for our
findings and conclusions based on our audit objectives. We believe that
the evidence obtained provides a reasonable basis for our findings and
conclusions based on our audit objectives.

Appendix II: UN Staff Assessment and the Tax Equalization Fund

As a part of its process for determining the base salary that an employee at each level receives, the United Nations (UN) deducts an amount, called the staff assessment, from the gross salary (see fig. 4). The UN deducts a higher staff assessment from staff members without dependents than from staff members with one or more dependents at the same grade and step. The staff assessment funds are credited to an account called the Tax Equalization Fund (TEF). Since policies regarding taxation of UN employees may vary among member states, the UN created the TEF as a means to reimburse staff members who are required to pay taxes to their home country and to equalize the net salaries of all UN staff members, regardless of their national tax obligations. Officials from the UN Secretariat's budget office said that currently the United States is the only country that requires its citizens employed at the UN to pay taxes on their UN earnings. Therefore, in practice, the TEF is used to reimburse Americans employed at the UN for the federal, state, and local income taxes they pay on their UN earnings. All other member states, which do not require their citizens to pay taxes on their UN earnings, receive a portion of the TEF as a credit toward their assessed dues to the UN budget.

Figure 4: UN Deducts the Staff Assessment from Gross Salaries

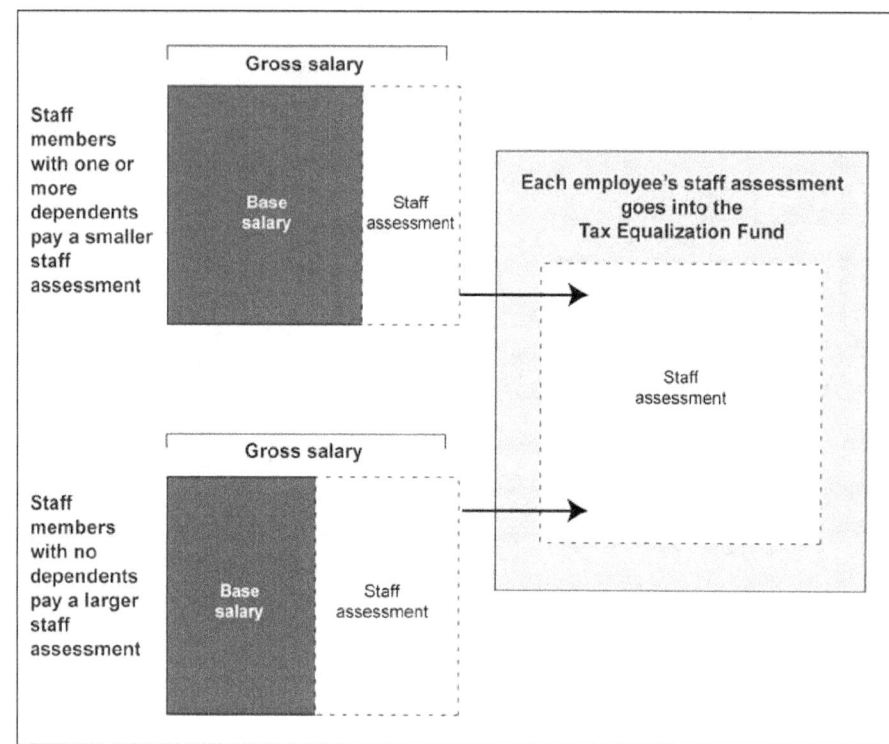

Source: GAO analysis based on ICSC documents.

The UN reviews staff assessment rates from time to time to ensure
sufficient funds are available to reimburse staff members for taxes paid or
to address any substantial increases in the fund. We previously reported
that the amount of credits in the TEF had increased significantly over the
period from 2002 to 2009.[1] As a result of this increase, the UN's budget
office requested that ICSC lower staff assessment rates. The General
Assembly approved ICSC's recommendation and the updated staff
assessment rates went into effect on January 1, 2012.

---

[1]GAO, *United Nations Renovations: Best Practices Could Enhance Future Cost Estimates*
GAO-12-795 (Washington, D.C.; July 25, 2012).

Appendix III: ICSC's Margin Calculation Process: Steps, Assumptions, and Alternatives

In this appendix, we describe in detail the ICSC margin calculation process and discuss the assumptions underlying the process, which we have determined are reasonable because they enable ICSC to compare UN and U.S. salaries, as required by the General Assembly. Further, we present a range of potential alternatives to these assumptions, which would also reasonably enable ICSC to compare UN and U.S. salaries.

Steps in ICSC's Net Salary Margin Calculation Process

ICSC has a complex, six-step process for calculating the margin, or difference between, the average net salaries of UN professional staff in New York City and U.S. civil service employees in Washington, D.C., which relies on a reasonable set of assumptions, as noted in this report. Figure 5 presents a flow chart illustrating the six steps of the margin calculation process.

Figure 5: Steps in the International Civil Service Commission's Net Salary Margin Calculation

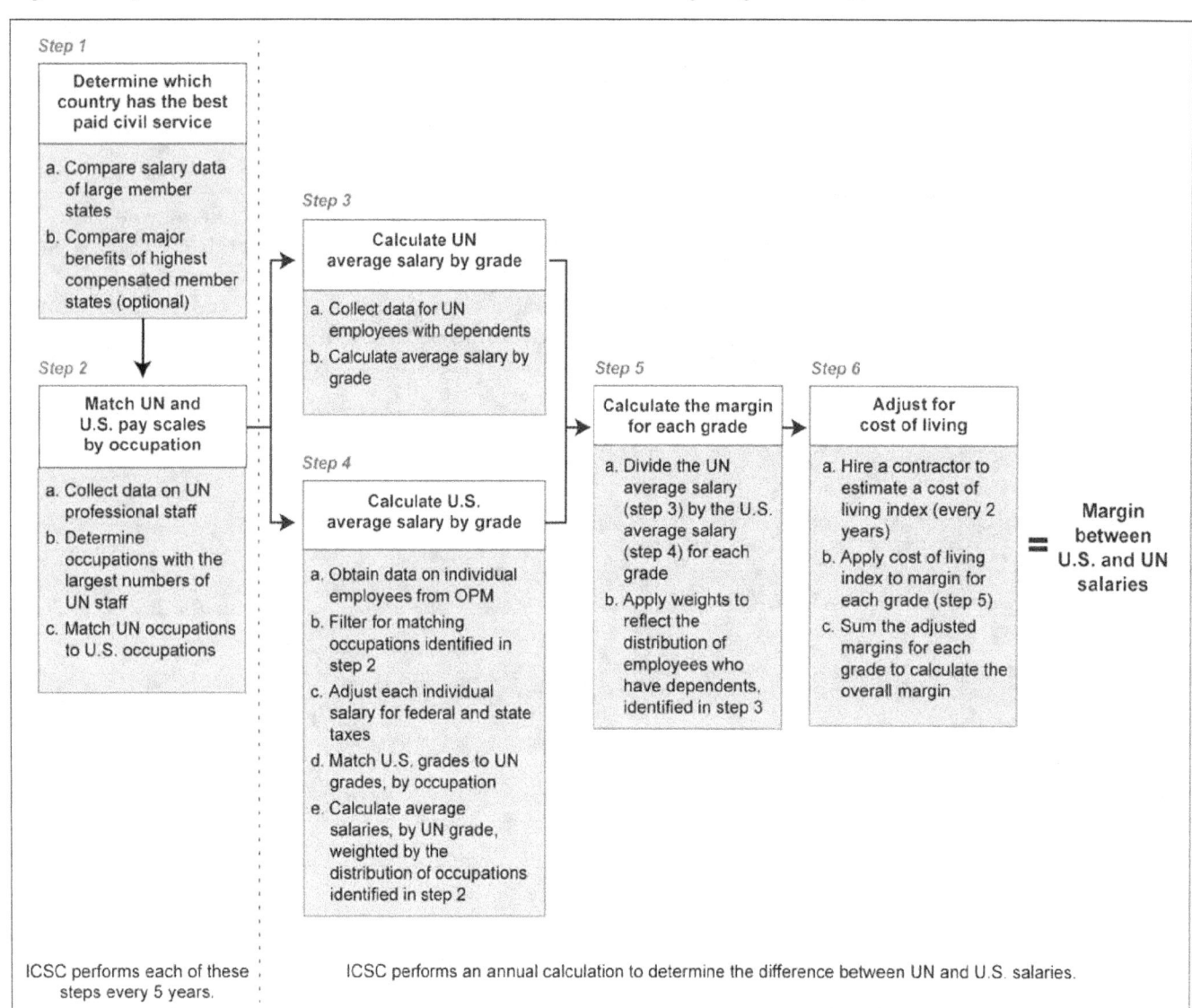

Source: GAO analysis based on ICSC documents.

Note: ICSC officials noted that some parts of steps 5 and 6 have been done in a different order, and not as completely separate steps. However, we found that the order of these steps does not change the calculated margin, and describing the steps separately increases the clarity of the process.

Step 1: Determine Which Country Has the Highest Compensated Civil Service

Since its founding, the UN has set salaries for professional staff according to the Noblemaire Principle, which states that employees' compensation should be set high enough to attract nationals from all member states, including those member states with the highest-compensated national civil service employees. In practice, ICSC has used net salary, rather than total compensation, to make this comparison in its annual margin calculation. Before ICSC can conduct the annual margin calculation, it must identify what it calls the comparator—the nation with the best-compensated civil service employees.[1] The General Assembly endorsed ICSC's recommendations to conduct a study to identify the comparator using a two-phase methodology. ICSC conducts the study, called the Noblemaire study, every 5 years.

Phase I of ICSC's methodology for the Noblemaire study reduces a list of candidate national civil services to a manageable number by comparing the average cash salaries of national civil service employees of selected nations. Only those nations deemed to have a reasonable possibility of replacing the current comparator are then considered for phase II, which involves the collection and evaluation of data on additional compensation elements.

ICSC begins phase I by identifying nations with a high enough level of economic resources to potentially qualify them as candidates to replace the United States as the comparator nation. For this step, it considers three sources of economic information: (1) the top 15 nations in per capita gross national income from a World Bank source, (2) the top 17 nations as determined by the U.S. Department of Labor based on per capita gross domestic product and employment rates, and (3) the 15 nations with the highest minimum wage according to the Global Wage Report from the International Labour Organization. ICSC selects for further consideration only nations that appear in at least two of these lists in phase I.

ICSC continues phase I by identifying nations with "significant numbers of staff at relevant levels." ICSC excludes nations with small numbers of civil service staff relative to the number of staff in the UN common system because it needs to compare similar occupations, and civil services with

---

[1]For the purposes of the Noblemaire study, compensation is measured as total net salary and the value of major additional benefits, including pension, health insurance, and life and accident insurance.

small numbers of staff are not likely to have sizable populations of the same types of occupations as the UN. After excluding nations with small civil services, ICSC reviews the pay structure of the remaining countries and also excludes systems whose pay structures are unlikely to be comparable to the UN professional grades.

ICSC completes phase I by comparing the after-tax cash salary, including any cash bonuses, of civil service employees at headquarters locations of each civil service. They compare a midpoint salary between the entry level and highest senior level salaries for each civil service, and adjust these midpoint salaries for cost of living and exchange rates in each headquarters location. On the basis of the results of this analysis, ICSC issues a report to the General Assembly as to whether any of the highest paid countries might qualify to replace the United States as the comparator and recommends whether phase II should be conducted for any country deemed a possible candidate to become the comparator.

Phase II, when conducted, is a seven-step process. First, ICSC obtains a sample of occupations in each civil service comparable to UN professional and higher categories, and classifies them according to the UN grading system. For these positions, ICSC quantifies the after-tax cash and non-cash compensation, including the estimated value of retirement benefits, health, life, and accident insurance benefits for each, and adjusts the resulting numbers for cost of living and exchange rates at headquarters locations. Finally, ICSC recommends that the General Assembly choose the comparator with the highest net compensation, based on its phase II calculation and other considerations, such as the cost of switching comparators. The General Assembly then decides whether the United States should remain the comparator or be replaced by a nation with higher net compensation for its national civil service employees.

Step 2: Match UN and U.S. Pay Scales by Occupation

Every 5 years, ICSC conducts a three-step grade equivalency study to determine which UN salary grades are equivalent to the civil service salary grades of the comparator. First, the UN's Chief Executives Board for Coordination (CEB) collects individual data on staff receiving the dependency rate salary from all UN common system organizations. Second, ICSC analyzes the UN staff data to determine the most populous occupations in the UN common system. ICSC officials said they aim to include occupations representing approximately 80 percent of all UN professional staff. Third, ICSC matches the most populous UN occupations to U.S. occupations. To do so, ICSC obtains data from the

Office of Personnel Management (OPM) on U.S. civil service staff living in the Washington, D.C., area and analyzes these data to determine likely occupation matches based on similar job titles and professional expertise. ICSC then analyzes job descriptors of these matches and applies UN criteria to determine how they would be graded under the UN system. Because these steps introduce an element of subjectivity, which could potentially threaten the validity of the results, ICSC has OPM check these determinations for validity against U.S. criteria. Finally, ICSC creates a grade equivalency matrix with the results, which shows for each specific occupation type in a U.S. grade how often it is classified in particular UN grades.[2]

Step 3: Calculate UN Average Salary by Grade

For the third step in the margin calculation, ICSC calculates the average salary of UN professional staff in New York by grade. To do so, ICSC first obtains data on all UN professional staff and then filters this data to match the assumptions of the previous steps. Specifically, ICSC filters out all staff who are not located in New York, then all employees who receive the single rate, and then employees who are not in the most populous occupations identified in the most recent grade equivalency study. Once ICSC has narrowed the data set through this filtering process, it calculates the average salary of professional staff in New York in each grade.

Step 4: Calculate U.S. Average Salary by Grade

For the fourth step in the margin calculation, ICSC calculates the average salary, after taxes, of U.S. civil service employees by grade. This step includes five substeps. First, ICSC purchases data each year from OPM that includes individual occupations, salaries, and General Service grade levels of U.S. civil service employees in Washington, D.C. Second, ICSC filter these data to include only occupations that appear in the most recent grade equivalency study. Third, ICSC treats all U.S. civil service employees as if they are married, filing jointly, and uses publicly available data on federal tax filings in Washington, D.C., Maryland, and Virginia to estimate the percentage of those tax filers in each of two groups: those who claim the standard deduction and those who itemize deductions. ICSC then applies these percentages to the OPM data on U.S. civil service employees in Washington, D.C., to estimate the number of

[2]U.S. grades include the General Schedule grades 9-15 and Senior Executive Service.

employees for each occupation type and grade that claim the standard deduction versus the number that itemize deductions. For the first group, ICSC determines the after-tax net salaries by subtracting the standard deduction, and for the second group, it subtracts the average itemized deduction. Third, using tax tables from Washington, D.C., Maryland, and Virginia, ICSC determines the net salaries after state taxes by subtracting the appropriate tax amount from each individual salary. Once these steps have been performed, ICSC uses the grade equivalency matrix to match the U.S. employee grade levels into the UN grade system. Finally, once distributed among UN grades, ICSC calculates the average salary, by UN grade.

Step 5: Calculate the Margin for Each Grade

ICSC calculates the ratios between UN professional staff in New York and U.S. civil service employees in Washington, D.C., for each grade, and adjusts those ratios to reflect the distribution of UN staff across grades from step 3 using weights based on the proportion of UN staff in each grade. Each of these ratios could be considered a margin for an individual grade. This is the simplest step of the margin calculation process, as the average UN salary in a grade is divided by the average U.S. salary in that grade, and then multiplied by the weight for that grade.

Step 6: Adjust for Cost of Living

Once the initial ratios are calculated, ICSC adjusts them based on the cost of living in the two headquarters locations. This adjustment is similar to the post adjustment, which also represents a cost of living estimate. ICSC hires an independent contractor to conduct a study of the cost of living in the two locations every 2 years. This contractor develops cost-of-living estimates based on several categories of spending that are common between the two populations in their respective locations, including selected goods and services, transportation, and housing. Ultimately, this study provides a single adjustment factor, which ICSC applies to each of the weighted average salary ratios from step 5. The adjustment factor, like the UN post adjustment, represents a measure of purchasing power. However, the post adjustment is developed using information from only UN employees, while this adjustment factor is based on information from a much larger population. Finally, after ICSC applies the cost-of-living adjustment factor to the average salary ratio for each grade, it calculates the overall margin by summing the adjusted ratio values for all grades.

Assumptions in ICSC's Margin Calculation Process

We determined that ICSC's margin calculation process relies on eight assumptions, each of which affects the annually calculated margin (see table 5). ICSC introduces two assumptions when conducting the Noblemaire study. First, ICSC assumes that civil service employees receive a similar amount of total national income across potential comparators. This assumption is implicit in the decision to use the measures of average per capita wages as an exclusion criterion in phase I of the study. Underlying these exclusion criteria is an assumption that general economic indicators are likely to identify the nations with the highest production and highest wages and that the nation with the highest compensated civil service would be found among them. However, because these criteria are not related directly to data on the salary received by civil service employees, it is possible that nations whose civil service salaries are high relative to the general population are being excluded. Second, by focusing comparisons on headquarters locations, ICSC assumes that employees in these locations are the most appropriate comparison group. According to ICSC officials, this assumption enables them to focus calculations on the locations with the most staff for each organization. For consistency, ICSC also limits its comparisons to the headquarters locations in steps 2 through 6 of the process.

Table 5: Assumptions the International Civil Service Commission Makes in the Margin Calculation Process

Steps	Assumption	Impact on margin calculation process
1	Per capita income is representative of civil service salaries in a country.	Potentially leads to exclusion of countries with civil service salaries that are outliers relative to their country's average, but provides a simple way to narrow the list of comparators.
1, 2, 3, 4, 5, 6	Employees in headquarters locations are representative of all employees.	Potentially excludes employees in locations that are outliers relative to headquarters, but reduces time and staff needed for step 6 while focusing on areas with the most employees.
2, 3, 4, 5	Employees receiving the dependency rate are representative of UN salary of all professional staff.	Excludes employees without dependents, who are paid lower salaries and who are more likely to be distributed at the lower UN grades, but prevents shocks in the annual margin calculation due to the greater stability of dependency rate employees.
2, 3, 4, 5	Occupations with the most staff are representative of all UN occupations.	Excludes employees in occupations with fewer staff who may be paid differently than those in more common occupations, but increases the likelihood that there are sufficient data to draw a comparison between UN and U.S. civil service employees.
3, 4, 5	The proportion of staff in each occupation is relatively stable for a 5-year period.	Includes occupations in the annual margin calculation that may have shrunk and excludes those that may have grown since the most recent grade equivalency study, but reduces the cost of conducting more frequent grade equivalency studies.
4, 5	All U.S. civil service employees are married and file jointly.	Decreases the accuracy of U.S. average net salary calculations, but enables ICSC to make a comparison despite limited data and uses the U.S. filing status that is most comparable to the UN dependency rate.
4, 5	U.S. civil service employees use the average deductions in their state.	Decreases the accuracy of U.S. average net salary calculations, but enables ICSC to make a comparison despite limited data on U.S. civil service employees' state income taxes.
6	Differences in salary between two locations are associated with the cost of living in those locations.	Margin comparison considers the purchasing power of employees rather than the cost of labor for those employees as in U.S. locality pay differentials, but the former is consistent with the UN's post adjustment.

Legend: Step 1 = Determine which country has the best paid civil service; Step 2 = Match UN and U.S. pay scales, by occupation; Step 3 = Calculate UN average salary by grade; Step 4 = Calculate U.S. average salary by grade; Step 5 = Calculate the margin for each grade; Step 6 = Adjust for cost of living.

Source: GAO analysis of ICSC source documents and interviews.

ICSC introduces two additional assumptions in the grade equivalency study. First, it assumes that employees receiving the dependent rate are the most appropriate population for this comparison of UN and U.S. salary grades. This assumption stems from ICSC's decision to limit the comparison to employees with dependents, and officials said it decreases the year-to-year volatility of the margin because it excludes single-rate employees. This assumption also applies to steps 3 through 5 of the margin calculation process. Second, ICSC assumes that the most populous occupations constitute the most appropriate population for the margin comparison. This assumption is also implicit and results from the decision to exclude populations with a small number of staff. This assumption reduces the time and staff needed to review job descriptors and generate the grade equivalency matrix. However, it also limits the occupations that can be considered in steps 3 through 5.

ICSC uses a fifth assumption in step three of its process. Specifically, ICSC assumes that the most populous occupations in the year of the margin calculation are similar to the most populous occupations in the most recent grade equivalency study. This assumption is unstated but is a result of the grade equivalency study being conducted every 5 years, and also applies to steps 4 and 5. By using this assumption, ICSC reduces the time and staff resources that would be needed for more frequent grade equivalency studies.

When calculating U.S. average salaries, ICSC introduces two more assumptions, both related to how ISCS adjusts U.S. gross salaries to net salaries after taxes. According to ICSC officials, these assumptions are necessary because ICSC does not have access to individual tax data for U.S. citizens. The first assumption is that all U.S. civil service employees file their taxes as married, filing jointly. The second is that the amount of those itemizing deductions is similar to the total population in their state of residence and that their average amount of deductions is likewise similar. ICSC uses the first assumption because the married, filing jointly tax status is the one most similar to the UN's salary rate for employees with dependents. ICSC uses the second assumption because this adjustment for the amount of taxes paid results in a more accurate average net salary than if no adjustment were used. Both of these assumptions affect the ratio calculations in step 5.

ICSC introduces an eighth assumption when it adjusts the ratios from step 5 for the cost of living. By choosing to use a cost of living adjustment, ICSC is implicitly assuming that any difference in salaries between two locations is a result of the cost of goods and services in those locations. This assumption is commonly used in economic analyses to control for cost differences in different locations and results in a more accurate margin calculation than if no adjustment were made.

Alternative Assumptions

As noted in this report, we determined that ICSC's assumptions were reasonable, but that other assumptions, which are also reasonable, would change the results. The alternative assumptions described in this section represent illustrative examples and are not intended to be a comprehensive list. Further, because any determination of the most appropriate alternative is dependent on the need for information to make decisions, and because member states and the General Assembly are ultimately the users of this information, we are not endorsing ICSC's assumptions or any of these alternatives as the most appropriate. Instead, we discuss the benefits and drawbacks of individual assumptions to present tradeoffs that could be considered by decision makers when deciding which assumptions are the most appropriate for their information needs.

ICSC's assumption that per capita income is representative of civil service salaries in a country is a low-cost way to reduce the number of countries for which it must do further calculations in the Noblemaire study because it allows for the use of readily available data and is at least somewhat related to the actual income of civil servants in those countries. However, this assumption may lead to the exclusion of outlier countries where civil services receive unusually high or low salaries, relative to the general population. To avoid the potential for unintentionally excluding countries that pay their civil service abnormally high salaries, ICSC could modify its exclusion criteria with some data related to actual government pay in member states, or by comparing cash compensation for civil service employees in all member states. The first option would maintain the benefit of requiring ICSC to compare only a subset of countries but may be more costly because data on government salaries in all countries are not readily available and might have to be gathered or purchased. The second option would guarantee that no countries are excluded unintentionally but would require ICSC to perform analysis on all member countries, which would likely be much more costly and time-consuming than the current approach because of both the lack of data from many countries and the magnitude of analysis that would be required.

ICSC's assumption that employees in headquarters locations are representative of all employees is beneficial because these locations tend to have a wide representation of occupations, and because limiting the comparison to two locations requires less time and staff resources than a comparison that includes all duty stations. However, if civil service staff outside of headquarters locations are systematically different from those in headquarters locations, this may reduce the accuracy of the margin calculation because the result may not be representative of all UN professional staff or of the entire civil service of the comparator. As one alternative, ICSC could choose to compare the UN and United States in a single location, which would simplify ICSC's process by eliminating the need for a cost-of-living adjustment, but which might reduce ICSC's ability to have a wide representation of occupations. As another alternative, ICSC could compare UN and U.S. employees in multiple locations, which would mitigate the risk of excluding or misrepresenting the respective staff but would increase the complexity of the process by requiring additional cost-of-living adjustments. This approach would also likely require increased time and resources to conduct the additional analysis.

According to ICSC officials, the assumption that employees receiving the dependent rate are the most appropriate population for the margin comparison has the benefit of increasing the stability of the margin calculation. However, this assumption leads to the exclusion of single-rate employees at the UN. As noted in our analysis of alternatives, ICSC could choose to include only single-rate employees, or they could choose to consider employees both with and without dependents. The first option could be beneficial if single-rate employees could be compared more directly to a particular U.S. tax filing status, but this option would also be limited because it would exclude employees with dependents. The second option would likely increase the accuracy of the margin calculation because no employees would be systematically excluded, but it could potentially result in more year-to-year fluctuation in the value of the margin, according to ICSC officials.

ICSC's assumption that the most populous occupations are the most appropriate population for the margin comparison also supports ICSC's goal of having stability in the calculation. This is because the average salaries of occupations with a low number of staff are affected more by an individual with a salary that is an outlier within the corresponding occupation and grade. However, as in the previous exclusion, this assumption further reduces the subset of employees included at the margin calculation. As an alternative, ICSC could determine grade equivalencies by including all employees in all occupations, which would result in a comparison of the full population of UN professional staff in New York with the full U.S. civil service in Washington, D.C. However, such a change would be more complex, costly, and time consuming than the current approach. According to ICSC officials, it could also result in less stability of the margin calculation over time.

ICSC assumes that the most populous occupations in the year of the margin calculation are similar to the most populous occupations in the most recent grade equivalency study. This assumption allows ICSC to conduct a grade equivalency study every 5 years. However, the distribution of occupations does change over time, and occasionally can do so abruptly. For example, ICSC said that some occupations, such as the position of librarian, have fallen off the list over time. As a result, in each year, the margin result reflects the difference in pay of occupations that were most populous in the year of the grade equivalency study, and not necessarily in the year of that specific margin calculation. ICSC could conduct the grade equivalency study less often, which might reduce the number of times such a study had to be paid for, but would also increase the likelihood that changes in the distribution of occupations are obscuring changes in the margin. ICSC could also choose to conduct the study more often, which would reduce this likelihood, but would also require the extra time and resources needed to conduct the study more frequently. ICSC could also perform some simplified analysis to assess whether the distribution of occupations has likely changed since the most recent grade equivalency study, which would provide a basis for deciding whether another study was needed. The costs and benefits of this option would depend on the complexity of this analysis, the cost of performing it, and the resulting frequency of grade equivalency studies.

ICSC's two assumptions about U.S. taxes are interrelated because both are a result of the data ICSC uses for the margin calculation. Because ICSC does not have data on the filing status of civil service employees, it assumes that everyone is married, filing jointly, and that they itemize their deductions at similar rates and in similar amounts to other employees in their state of residence. These assumptions enable a comparison with the UN dependent-rate employees, but because ICSC has not validated the assumptions against actual tax filing data of U.S. civil service employees, its estimates of tax liabilities may not be accurate. ICSC could attempt to obtain data on the filing status and amounts paid by U.S. civil service staff; however, it is likely that these data would be restricted from ICSC due to privacy concerns, or could be costly to procure.

ICSC assumes that a comparison of purchasing power, as defined by the cost of living, is the most appropriate measure for comparing the salaries of the two populations. This assumption is consistent with the UN post adjustment system, which seeks to equalize purchasing power across UN posts and is commonly used to control for differences in the cost of living in two locations. However, a cost-of-labor measure, such as the locality pay system used by the U.S. civil service, could be a reasonable alternative. As with cost of living, cost of labor is commonly used to control for differences in wages in two locations. Using the U.S. locality pay adjustments would have the benefit that it could be done at a lower cost, as opposed to ICSC's current practice of contracting an independent study, but would have the drawback of being a departure from the UN's practice of using cost of living in its pay-setting process.

Appendix IV: UN and U.S. Civil Service Retirement Benefits

	United Nations	United States Civil Service
Retirement age (normal retirement and early retirement)	Normal retirement age is 60 for employees who began working at the UN before January 1, 1990. Normal retirement age is 62 for employees who began working at the UN after January 1, 1990. Participants whose age at separation is at least 55 years but less than normal retirement age and have at least 5 years of service are eligible for a reduced retirement benefit The retirement age for UN employees hired on or after January 1, 2014, is 65.	Under the Civil Service Retirement System (CSRS), full retirement age is 55 with 30 years of service, age 60 with 20 years of service, or age 62 with 5 years of service. CSRS participants who retire before age 55 are eligible for a reduced retirement benefit. For Federal Employee Retirement System (FERS) employees, normal retirement age is 60 with at least 20 years of service or 62 with at least 5 years of service. A person with 30 years or more of service may retire earlier; the minimum retirement age ranges from 55 to 57. A FERS employee at the minimum retirement age is eligible to retire with at least 10, but less than 30 years of service, at a reduced benefit. For both CSRS and FERS, employees may retire early for involuntary separations or during major reorganizations or reductions in force. For CSRS, employees can retire early at any age with 25 years of service. For FERS, employees can retire at age 50 with 20 years of service, or at any age with 25 years of service.
Retirement contribution	The current rate of contribution to the Fund is 23.7 percent of pensionable remuneration. The employee pays 1/3, or 7.9 percent, of that amount. The UN pays the remaining 2/3, or 15.8 percent.	Most CSRS employees contribute 7 percent of their salary and the employer contributes a matching amount. In fiscal year 2012, FERS employees contributed 0.8 percent of their salary and the employer paid 11.9 percent, for a total of 12.7 percent. As of January 1, 2013, newly hired employees covered by FERS must contribute 3.1 percent and the employer contribution is 9.6 percent. FERS employees also contribute to the Defined Contribution Plan (Thrift Savings Plan). Certain groups of federal employees have different retirement contribution levels under CSRS and FERS. Law enforcement officers and firefighters, congressional employees, members of congress, bankruptcy judges, judges of the United States Court of Military Appeals, and United States magistrates have higher contribution rates.

	United Nations	**United States Civil Service**
Retirement benefit	For employees who reach full retirement age and have at least 5 years of service, the annual pension is calculated as 1.5 percent of the final average remuneration for each of the first 5 years of service, plus 1.75 percent of the final average remuneration for each of the next 5 years of service, plus 2 percent of the final average remuneration for each year of service between year 10 and year 35 of service; plus an additional 1 percent of final average remuneration for any years of service above 35, up to a maximum total accumulation rate of 70 percent of final average remuneration. Final average remuneration generally means the highest average salary (or pensionable remuneration) for 36 months of the last 5 years of service.	CSRS employee annual retirement benefit is calculated as 1.5 percent of the high three salary for each of the first 5 years of service, plus 1.75 percent of the high 3 salary for each of the next 5 years of service, plus 2 percent of the high-three salary for each year of service beyond year 10, up to a maximum of 80 percent of the high-three salary plus credit for unused sick leave. The high-three salary is defined as the highest average salary over any contiguous 3-year period of service. For FERS employees age 62 or older, and with 20 years or more of service, the annual retirement benefit is calculated as 1.1 percent of the high-three salary for each year of service. For FERS employees retiring earlier than age 62 or with less than 20 years of service, the annual retirement benefit is 1 percent of the high-three salary for each year of service.
Defined contribution plan	No UN equivalent	Thrift Savings Plan (TSP) CSRS: Employees may contribute income to TSP up to federal limit. Government does not match contributions. FERS: Government contributes 1 percent of pay automatically to TSP. Employees may contribute pre-or post-tax income to TSP up to the federal limit ($17,500 in 2013). The government matches up to 4 percent.
Disability benefit	Disability benefits payable when a participant cannot perform his or her duties because of injury or illness of permanent or long duration.	CSRS: Employees are eligible for disability retirement at any age, with at least 5 years of service. Employees must have a disability expected to last at least 1 year. FERS: Employees are eligible for disability retirement at any age, with at least 18 months of service. Employees must have a disability expected to last at least 1 year.
Widow and widower benefit	Widow and widower benefits payable to surviving spouse if participant was entitled to retirement benefits or died while in service.	A monthly survivor annuity is available to employees who have worked for at least 18 months, were covered by FERS/CSRS and provided that the widow/widower meets certain conditions. Note: The spouse of a FERS-covered employee may be eligible for the Basic Employee Death Benefit, which is equal to 50 percent of the employee's final salary (average salary, if higher), plus $15,000. The $15,000 has increased to $30,792.98 for deaths on or after December 1, 2011.
Dependent children benefits	Benefits payable to dependent children of employees who are entitled to retirement or disability benefits or who died while in service. Benefits paid up to age 21. Benefits are payable to a dependent child over 21 if child is incapacitated by illness or injury.	Unmarried children who are dependent upon the employee/annuitant may receive monthly benefits until they reach age 18, marry, or die. Monthly survivor annuity payments for a child can continue after age 18, if the child is a full-time student attending a recognized school. Benefits can continue until age 22.
Secondary dependent benefits	Secondary dependent benefits payable to a survivor, such as mother or father, of an employee who was entitled to retirement benefits and died in service.	If the employee has no spouse or children, a payment may be made to the employee's parents, the administrator of the employee's estate, or next of kin as determined in the laws of the employee's state.

Source: GAO analysis of UN and Office of Personnel Management data.

Note:

[a]CSRS generally applied to employees hired before 1984. FERS generally applies to employees first hired after 1984.

Appendix V: UN Allowances and Allowances for U.S. Civil Service Staff Serving Overseas and Foreign Service Officers

	UN	US Civil Service Employees Serving Overseas and Foreign Service Officers
Housing Subsidy	UN employees are eligible for a rental subsidy intended to provide equity in accommodation expenses among UN staff in duty stations where rents vary considerably; and to alleviate hardships staff may face if their rent is higher than average for reasonable standard accommodations. For duty stations in Europe and North America, the UN determines a reasonable maximum rent level (or ceiling) that is used to determine how much an employee should pay, taking into account their rent, their income, and whether they have dependents. Newly hired staff are eligible to receive a subsidy for the portion of their rent that exceeds the reasonable maximum. They can receive the subsidy for up to 7 years, and it declines over time. In years 1 through 4, the subsidy is 80 percent, in year 5 the subsidy is 60 percent, in year 6 it is 40 percent, and in year 7 it is 20 percent For duty stations outside Europe and North America, the standard rental subsidy is 80 percent of the rent exceeding the threshold, up to a maximum of 40 percent of rent.	U.S. civilian employees are eligible for housing subsidies, called quarters allowances, that are designed to reimburse employees for substantially all costs of residing in either temporary or permanent living quarters. A quarters allowance is not granted when government housing is provided. A temporary quarters subsistence allowance is granted to an employee for the reasonable cost of temporary quarters, meals, and laundry expenses incurred by the employee and/or family member at the foreign post upon initial arrival or preceding final departure. A living quarters allowance is granted to an employee for the annual cost of suitable, adequate living quarters for the employee and his or her family. An extraordinary quarters allowance is granted to an employee who must vacate permanent quarters due to renovations, or unhealthy or dangerous conditions.
Cost of living (exclusive of quarters cost)	The UN pays a post adjustment to employees to ensure equity in purchasing power of staff members across duty stations. The post adjustment is a part of the employee's salary and is not considered an allowance. The post adjustment is higher for employees with dependents.	The U.S. government grants a post allowance to employees officially stationed at a post in a foreign area where the cost of living is substantially higher than in Washington, D.C. The post allowance is designed to permit employees to spend the same portion of their salaries for their standard living expenses as they would if they were residing in Washington, D.C. The amount paid is a flat rate that varies by basic salary, size of family, and post.
Relocation expenses	UN employees are eligible for an assignment grant that is intended to provide staff with a reasonable cash amount at the beginning of the assignment for the costs incurred as a result of appointment or reassignment. The amount of the grant varies by duty station and whether the employee has dependents. For example, a staff member with two dependents assigned to headquarters for a period of 2 years might earn an assignment grant of $7,200 to compensate for 30 days at the beginning of the assignment. The UN also pays removal and shipment costs for employees. Employees may ship personal effects only, or household goods and personal effects in some cases. The UN has established weight limits for this allowance, which depend on the employee's number of dependents.	The U.S. government grants a foreign transfer allowance to employees for extraordinary, necessary, and reasonable expenses, incurred by an employee transferring to any post of assignment in a foreign area, prior to departure. This allowance includes a miscellaneous expense portion, a wardrobe expense portion, a pre-departure subsistence expense portion, and a lease penalty expense portion. The U.S. government offers a home service transfer allowance for extraordinary, necessary, and reasonable expenses for employees prior to transferring back to a post in the United States. This allowance includes a miscellaneous expense portion, a wardrobe expense portion, a subsistence expense portion, and a lease penalty expense portion.

	UN	US Civil Service Employees Serving Overseas and Foreign Service Officers
Maintaining family at separate location	For a UN staff member located in a duty station that lacks appropriate schools and medical facilities to meet family members' needs, and who is obliged to pay rent in another city for their family, the staff member's rent at the duty station and the rent for the family in the capital city can be considered one combined rent for the purposes of determining the rental subsidy.	The U.S. government offers a separate maintenance allowance to assist an employee who is required to maintain family members at locations other than his/her overseas post of assignment either due to (a) dangerous, notably unhealthful, or excessively adverse living conditions at the post; (b) because of special needs or hardship involving the employee or family member; (c) if the family needs to stay temporarily in commercial quarters, such as a hotel.
Education allowance	UN employees serving outside their home country are eligible for an education grant to cover part of the cost of educating children in full-time attendance at an educational institution. The amount of the grant is equivalent to 75 percent of allowable costs, subject to a maximum that varies from country to country. Employees are eligible for the grant up to the fourth year of their child's postsecondary education, or age 25. For U.N. employees in the United States, the maximum education grant in August 2012 was $32,255. At designated locations where educational facilities are inadequate, UN also covers up to 100 percent of boarding costs, up to a maximum amount, for children at the primary or secondary level, in addition to the standard maximum amount of education grant.	The U.S. government provides an allowance to assist an employee in meeting the extraordinary and necessary expenses in providing adequate elementary and secondary education for dependent children at an overseas post of assignment. The amount of the grant depends on whether the child is in a school at post, at a school away from the post, or in home study or at a private institution.
Educational travel	In addition to the educational allowance, UN employees are entitled to travel expenses for their child for one return journey from the educational institution to their duty station, if the educational institution is outside the country of the duty station. At some duty stations, the UN allows an additional round-trip journey in a non-home leave year.	The U.S. government pays the expenses for a child to travel to and from a secondary school or post-secondary school, once each way annually. The age limitation for secondary education travel is 20 (before the 21st birthday), and for post-secondary education the age limitation is 22 (before the 23rd birthday).
Danger pay allowance	The UN provides a special allowance for staff required to work under dangerous conditions. The danger pay is granted for up to 3 months at a time, subject to ongoing review. For internationally recruited staff, the allowance is $1,600 per month. For locally recruited staff, the allowance is based on the local salary scale.	The U.S. government provides additional compensation of up to 35 percent over basic compensation to employees, for service at places in foreign areas where dangerous conditions that could threaten the health or well being of an employee exist.
Representation allowance	No comparable allowance.	The U.S. government provides an allowance intended to cover expenditures by employees when these expenditures are made to help establish and maintain relationships of value to the U.S. in foreign countries. The allowance covers expenses such as entertainment of a protocol nature; purchases of flowers, wreaths, or other tokens made in accordance with local custom; or printing, engraving, or purchasing of invitations to official functions.
Official residence expenses	No comparable allowance.	The U.S. government provides an allowance to assist principal representatives with the unusual expenses that they incur in the operation and maintenance of a suitable official residence.

	UN	US Civil Service Employees Serving Overseas and Foreign Service Officers
Advance of pay	No comparable allowance.	The head of an agency may provide for the advance payment of up to 3 months pay to or for the account of an employee proceeding to or arriving at a post of assignment in the foreign area. Advance of pay may also be paid for certain medical emergencies.
Rest and recuperation travel	No comparable allowance.	The United States may grant Foreign Service employees and their eligible family members rest and recuperation travel to the United States, its territories, or other locations abroad.
Children's allowance	The UN provides eligible staff members an annual children's allowance of $2,929 per child under age 18 or under 21 if a full-time student). Staff without a dependent spouse do not receive a children's allowance for their first dependent child.	No comparable allowance.
Mobility allowance	To encourage movement from one duty station to another, the UN provides an annual mobility allowance to staff on an assignment of 1 year or more who have had 5 consecutive years of service in the UN system. The amount of this allowance varies by the employee's number of assignments, duty station, and whether the employee has dependents. As of August 2012, this allowance ranged from $1,970 to $16,490.	No comparable allowance.
Hardship allowance	The UN provides an annual hardship allowance to staff on assignment in duty stations where living and working conditions are difficult. The hardship allowance varies by position level and dependency status. The allowance varies depending on the employee's duty station, salary level, and whether the employee has dependents. As of August 2012, the allowance ranged from $4,360 to $22,680.	The U.S. government provides a post hardship differential, which is additional compensation of 25, 30, or 35 percent of salary to employees for service at places in foreign areas where conditions of environment differ substantially from conditions of environment in the continental United States and warrant additional compensation as a recruitment and retention incentive. A hardship differential is established for locations where the living conditions are extraordinarily difficult, involve excessive physical hardship, or are notably unhealthy. A U.S. government agency may also grant a difficult-to-staff incentive differential to employees assigned to a hardship post upon a determination that additional pay is warranted to recruit and retain employees at that post. The allowance is an additional 15 percent of salary.
Travel expenses	The UN pays travel expenses for employees when they are initially appointed, when they change their duty station, when they separate from service, when they travel on official business, when they travel for home leave, and when they travel to visit family members. The UN pays travel expenses for employee dependents on the initial appointment, on separation from service, and on education grant travel and home leave. Employees also receive a daily allowance while on travel.	The State Department pays travel and related expenses for members of the Foreign Service and their families under a number of circumstances, including when they are proceeding to and returning from assigned posts of duty; for authorized or required home leave; for family members to accompany, precede, or follow a foreign service member to a place of temporary duty; for representation travel; medical travel; rest and recuperation travel; evacuation travel; or other travel as authorized.[a]

	UN	US Civil Service Employees Serving Overseas and Foreign Service Officers
Home leave	The UN offers employees who are posted outside their home country paid travel to their home country every 2 years. This includes travel for the employee and the employee's dependents. No additional annual leave is granted for this purpose, but reasonable time off is given to cover the duration of travel between the duty station and the place of home leave. Home leave may be granted every 12 months at some duty stations.	The Foreign Service Act of 1980 requires home leave for all employees following completion of 3 years continuous service abroad. In some cases, home leave must be taken after 12 months of service. The purpose of home leave is to ensure that employees who live abroad for an extended period undergo reorientation and re-exposure in the United States on a regular basis; it is not considered an employee benefit.[a]
Family visit travel	The UN may pay for the travel of an employee to visit a family member if none of the employee's eligible family members have travelled to the duty station at the organization's expense during the preceding 12 months. Employees may take family visit travel every other year, provided it takes place in the non-home leave year.	Foreign service employees assigned to some hardship posts receive family visit travel. This travel permits a member to visit family who would reside at post with the member if the post were not within a hostile area at which family members cannot reside. In addition, the U.S. government offers emergency visitation travel, which pays for the employee to travel from their post to the United States or to other locations in case of a family emergency.[a]
Transportation of an automobile	The UN pays part of the cost of transporting an employee's privately owned automobile to some duty stations outside of Europe and the United States.	No comparable allowance.

Source: GAO analysis of UN and Office of Personnel Management data.

Note:

[a]The information for this allowance is relevant to Foreign Service Officers only.

Appendix VI: Comments from the Department of State

Note: GAO comments supplementing those in the report text appear at the end of this appendix.

United States Department of State

Comptroller
1969 Dyess Avenue
Charleston, SC 29405

MAY 1 3 2013

Dr. Loren Yager
Managing Director
International Affairs and Trade
Government Accountability Office
441 G Street, N.W.
Washington, D.C. 20548-0001

Dear Dr. Yager:

We appreciate the opportunity to review your draft report, "UN COMPENSATION: United Nations Should Clarify the Process and Assumptions Underlying Secretariat Professional Salaries" GAO Job Code 320935.

The enclosed Department of State comments are provided for incorporation with this letter as an appendix to the final report.

If you have any questions concerning this response, please contact Matt Glockner, Program Analyst, Bureau of International Organization Affairs at (202) 647-6413.

Sincerely,

James L. Millette

cc: GAO – Thomas Melito
        IO – Dr. Esther D. Brimmer
        State/OIG – Evelyn Klemstine

Department of State Comments on GAO Draft Report

UN COMPENSATION: United Nations Should Clarify the Process and Assumptions Underlying Secretariat Professional Salaries (GAO-13-526, GAO Code 320935)

Thank you for the opportunity to comment on your draft report entitled *UN COMPENSATION: United Nations Should Clarify the Process and Assumptions Underlying Secretariat Professional Salaries.* The Department of State notes that GAO was requested to explain how the UN sets salaries for its professional staff and to compare compensation (salaries, benefits, and allowances) for UN professional staff and U.S. federal civil servants and believes that the GAO report provides timely and useful information that will support our efforts to make sure UN compensation can attract and retain talent meeting the highest standards of efficiency, competence, and integrity while ensuring fiscal discipline at the UN.

The Department of State recalls that the UN sets salaries in accordance with the Noblemaire Principle. The Noblemaire Principle requires salaries for UN professional staff to be set in comparison to the highest-paid national civil service. Since 1945, this has been the U.S. federal civil service. The UN uses a complex methodology to compare salaries for each and make sure that salaries for UN professional staff stay between 110% and 120% of salaries for U.S. federal civil service.

The GAO report notes that the comparison methodology is complex and not clearly communicated to UN member states. The Department of State generally endorses this conclusion and accepts the GAO recommendation to work with other member states to request the International Civil Service Commission (ICSC) to clarify the methodology and its assumptions to facilitate more effective oversight by member states.

See comment 1.

On salaries for UN professional staff, the Department of State notes other areas for study that we believe can inform our engagement on UN compensation matters in the future. We found the section in the GAO report on alternative assumptions for the comparison methodology particularly interesting, and we believe that it would have been useful if the report had expressed an opinion on which of the alternative assumptions tested is optimal. We also believe that it would have been useful for the report to examine the justification for setting the margin at 110-120% as opposed to a lower range.

See comment 2.

The GAO report presents clear and concise information about the benefits and allowances for UN professional staff but the Department of State notes that further study of the comparison between benefits and allowances packages for UN professional staff and U.S. federal civil servants could also inform our engagement. We agree with the GAO assessment that UN professional staff and U.S. federal civil servants get similar types of benefits and allowances. Like all U.S. civil servants, UN professional staff receive annual and sick leave, retirement benefits, and life and health insurance. Also, UN professional staff are eligible for the same allowances as U.S. federal civil servants serving overseas (e.g., education grant and rental subsidy). We believe that it would have been useful for the report to quantify the differences in benefits and allowances to help us understand whether <u>total</u> compensation for UN professional staff and U.S. federal civil servants are aligned. It would have also been useful for the report to attempt a direct comparison between salaries, benefits, and allowances as a whole.

The Department of State remains committed to working with ICSC and other member states to make further progress on improving transparency of the calculations for UN professional staff compensation. The United States has led the charge to clarify the methodology used to set and adjust UN salaries and benefits. Due to lobbying by the United States and other member states, the Fifth Committee of the UN General Assembly recently requested a comprehensive review of the UN compensation package and the underlying methodology behind it. The intent of this review is to recommend to the General Assembly what is needed to attract and retain talent while taking into account that UN organizations face financial constraints and recommend ways to streamline the methodology to make it more clear and accountable to member state oversight.

The following are GAO's comments on the State Department's letter
dated May 13 2013.

GAO Comments

1. As we note in the report, member states and the General Assembly
   are the ultimate users of this information, and are best suited to select
   the approach that is the most appropriate for their needs, which is why
   we do not specifically endorse any of the alternatives. The report is
   intended to provide information on how ICSC calculates the margin
   between UN and U.S. civil service salaries. Member states may be
   able to use the information in this report as they deliberate on whether
   to approve ICSC's recommendations to change UN salaries each
   year. Regarding the margin, the General Assembly made the
   decision that average UN net salaries should fall within a 110 to 120
   percent of average U.S. civil service net salaries. It is outside of the
   scope of our review to examine the justification for the General
   Assembly's decision.

2. We plan to provide more in-depth information about the value of UN
   and U.S. civil service employee benefits and allowances in a
   forthcoming report.

Appendix VII: Comments from the United Nations

Note: GAO comments supplementing those in the report text appear at the end of this appendix.

UNITED NATIONS   NATIONS UNIES

INTERNATIONAL CIVIL SERVICE   COMMISSION DE LA FONCTION
COMMISSION   PUBLIQUE INTERNATIONALE

Two United Nations Plaza, 10th Floor,   New York, NY 10017
Fax: (212) 963-0159 / 963-1717, Tel: (212) 963-8464

Office of the Chairman   Bureau du Président

Reference: ICSC 60-40-1-6   13 May 2013

Dear Mr. Melito,

   We thank you for affording us the opportunity of providing our views on the draft GAO Report (May 2013) on UN Compensation.   We worked closely with the GAO team from the beginning of their assignment to provide them with all of the information they requested and granted them open access to our data. Along the way, we held in-depth discussions and provided a wealth of explanatory material both in writing and by teleconferencing to correct and clear up misunderstandings and misconceptions about how the UN compensation system functions. We hope that these corrections will find their way into the final Report. At this stage of the report process we will limit ourselves to some general comments aimed at facilitating a better understanding of the way the International Civil Service Commission carries out its mandate, and more specifically on the perception that our reports to the General Assembly lack clarity and transparency, particularly with regard to the calculation of the net UN/US remuneration margin.

   It is recalled that when the General Assembly established the ICSC as its subsidiary expert body and adopted its statute, it assigned to the Commission a set of specific responsibilities. It also differentiated between matters for which the authority was entrusted to the Commission and those on which the Assembly would decide. So, while the General Assembly decides on the broad principles for the determination of the conditions of service of the staff, the Commission establishes the methods by which these principles should be applied. In the case of the net remuneration margin, the Commission elaborated a methodology which was approved by the Assembly. ICSC has consistently continued to apply that methodology and the Assembly has consistently continued to endorse it.

   The Commission has always endeavoured to provide in its annual reports to the General Assembly the necessary and appropriate amount of information required for Member States to understand its recommendations and decisions, particularly those of a technical nature, all the

Mr. Thomas Melito
Director, International Affairs and Trade
Government Accountability Office
Washington, D.C.

2

See comment 1.

while confining the length of its reports to the stringent documentation limits established by the Assembly. The Commission seems to be caught between the horns of a dilemma, receiving criticism from some quarters for its perceived lack of clarity and failure to provide sufficient comprehensive information on the highly complex and technical subjects for which it is responsible, and from other quarters, complaints that its annual reports are too long, too technical and too complex to be easily understood. The ever changing composition and turnover of Member State delegations responsible for ICSC reports presents its own particular challenge.

That is why it has been long-standing practice to complement the Commission's report with additional information, both in the form of written supplementary papers and oral briefings, on any item deemed necessary by the Assembly. The Commission's secretariat arranges on a regular basis for in-depth presentations, either on its own initiative or at the request of the Fifth Committee. Further, the Commission's decisions on all major items are summarized in the Commission's compendium which is posted and regularly updated on the Commission website. We therefore consider that the information provided to the Assembly is both transparent and comprehensive and that we have done our best to facilitate and enhance understanding through supplementary briefings and presentations given the highly technical nature of some of the items.

Turning to the net remuneration margin, we were pleased to note recognition in the draft Report that the GAO team found the assumptions used by the ICSC in that calculation to be reasonable. These are the same underlying assumptions that have been relied upon over the years to calculate a margin that, as noted above, has heretofore met with the Assembly's approbation.

See comment 1.

We would add that while all of the information related to the calculation of the margin may not be available in a single document, all relevant information is in fact reported to the Commission and/or the General Assembly—most of which was given to the audit team. It is worth recalling that the legislative base of this particular matter, like many others in the UN, is a dynamic one. It is not a static process, but one which is constantly evolving, with new resolutions and decisions coming forward at least on an annual basis. A complex matter such as the net remuneration margin requires review and consideration of actions taken by the Assembly and the Commission over time (i.e., a span of years) in order to have a full understanding of the underlying process and rationale of the decisions.

See comment 2.

Now to some specific points that were either mentioned, or omitted, in the draft Report. One of the alternative scenarios put forward by the GAO team uses cost of labour indicators instead of a cost of living factor, though the team understood that such an approach would not be compatible with the post adjustment system, one of the underpinning elements of the UN remuneration system. The UN salary system of necessity must equalize the purchasing power of salaries across the world in order to maintain the principle of equal pay for work of equal value.

Further, the Commission has long felt frustrated by its inability to gain access to a key element of the margin calculation—data on pay systems other than the General Schedule and the Senior Executive Service. Data gaps as significant as these may hinder the ability of the

See comment 3.

See comment 4.

See comment 5.

3

Commission to estimate the margin as accurately as it would like. By some accounts, including a 2007 study on the characteristics and pay of the Federal civilian employees by the Congressional Budget Office, the absence of data on these systems may have a distorting effect on the UN/US margin comparison. This is a critical example of a key lacuna which is not addressed in the GAO draft Report.

We also note that the United States civil service has a number of added pay flexibilities including recruitment, retention and relocation allowances, a difficult-to-staff incentive differential housing supplements for some employees assigned to high-cost locations within the US and a student loan repayment program, in addition to the benefits offered to expatriate employees in the United States civil service. These top-ups are significant features of the United States remuneration package and should be indicated in the broader summary table presented in the GAO report even if they are not used in the United Nations/United States comparisons.

Lastly, the reference to the *Standards for Internal Controls in the Federal Government* implies a responsibility on the part of ICSC to comply with US standards for information. Clearly, this is not the case and, as already noted, we are confident that our methodology is transparent and has been both fully described and fully explained.

In closing, we would like to express our appreciation for the understanding and cooperation shown by the GAO team in carrying out this review.

Yours sincerely,

Kingston Rhodes

The following are GAO's comments on ICSC's letter dated May 13, 2013.

GAO Comments

1. While ICSC notes that it faces challenges in reporting on its highly complex and technical process for calculating the margin between UN and U.S. salaries, nevertheless, ICSC can, though supplementary reports and oral briefings, provide more clarity on this process to the General Assembly. As we reported, representatives from several member states said that they did not understand the margin calculation process. Further, as ICSC points out in their letter, there is no single document that provides all the relevant information about the margin calculation. As we described in Appendix I of our report, we reviewed numerous documents to try to gain a clear understanding of the margin calculation process. We also supplemented the data ICSC provided with published information we obtained independently and some additional data from the UN Chief Executives' Board in order to replicate some parts of their process. However, we were not able to fully describe ICSC's margin calculation until we met several times with ICSC officials to clarify various aspects of the process. We believe that more clarity is needed about the margin calculation process and its underlying assumptions to better inform member states, so that they can effectively oversee ICSC's process for setting and adjusting salaries and ensure that its work is in line with the General Assembly resolution.

2. In our report, we noted the ICSC utilizes cost-of-living measures for two different purposes: when it sets the post adjustment for each duty station, and when it compares UN salaries in New York to U.S. civil service salaries in Washington D.C. We do not question the ICSC's use of a cost-of-living measure to set the post adjustment to equalize the purchasing power of UN Secretariat salaries. However, the UN's remuneration system is based on the Noblemaire Principle, and in practice the UN bases its salaries on the U.S. civil service; thus it is reasonable to note that the United States uses a cost-of-labor factor in setting its locality pay adjustments when comparing New York and Washington, D.C. Using this measure, we calculated a margin of 126.7, which is outside the margin range of 110 to 120 percent.

3. This issue is outside the scope of our review. ICSC officials we met with noted that their process generally is based on the U.S. General Schedule and that they request information on other pay scales. We have added a footnote to the report to reflect ICSC's comment.

4. Appendix V of the report discusses allowances such as difficult-to-staff incentives and housing supplements offered under the

Department of State's Standardized Regulations. We plan to provide more in-depth information about other allowances, such as student loan reimbursement, in a forthcoming report.

5. We agree that ICSC does not have to comply with U.S. federal internal control standards, however, we cite our own standards for internal control as a best practice and note that key information should be recorded and communicated to management and others within the entity who need it, and in a form and within a time frame that enables them to carry out their internal control and other responsibilities. Without such information, member states cannot effectively evaluate whether ICSC's process best satisfies the General Assembly resolution. Our recommendation is that State and the U.S. Mission to the UN should work with other member states to make sure that they can get the information they need for effective oversight of ICSC's process.

Appendix VIII: GAO Contact and Staff Acknowledgments

GAO Contact	Thomas Melito, (202) 512-9601 or melitot@gao.gov
Staff Acknowledgments	In addition to the staff named above, Valérie Nowak (Assistant Director), Diana Blumenfeld, Debbie Chung, David Dayton, Leah DeWolf, Mark Dowling, Etana Finkler, Joy Labez, Erin McLaughlin, Rhiannon Patterson, Steven Putansu, Jeremy Sebest and Roberta G. Steinman made significant contributions to this report.

GAO's Mission	The Government Accountability Office, the audit, evaluation, and investigative arm of Congress, exists to support Congress in meeting its constitutional responsibilities and to help improve the performance and accountability of the federal government for the American people. GAO examines the use of public funds; evaluates federal programs and policies; and provides analyses, recommendations, and other assistance to help Congress make informed oversight, policy, and funding decisions. GAO's commitment to good government is reflected in its core values of accountability, integrity, and reliability.
Obtaining Copies of GAO Reports and Testimony	The fastest and easiest way to obtain copies of GAO documents at no cost is through GAO's website (http://www.gao.gov). Each weekday afternoon, GAO posts on its website newly released reports, testimony, and correspondence. To have GAO e-mail you a list of newly posted products, go to http://www.gao.gov and select "E-mail Updates."
Order by Phone	The price of each GAO publication reflects GAO's actual cost of production and distribution and depends on the number of pages in the publication and whether the publication is printed in color or black and white. Pricing and ordering information is posted on GAO's website, http://www.gao.gov/ordering.htm. Place orders by calling (202) 512-6000, toll free (866) 801-7077, or TDD (202) 512-2537. Orders may be paid for using American Express, Discover Card, MasterCard, Visa, check, or money order. Call for additional information.
Connect with GAO	Connect with GAO on Facebook, Flickr, Twitter, and YouTube. Subscribe to our RSS Feeds or E-mail Updates. Listen to our Podcasts. Visit GAO on the web at www.gao.gov.
To Report Fraud, Waste, and Abuse in Federal Programs	Contact: Website: http://www.gao.gov/fraudnet/fraudnet.htm E-mail: fraudnet@gao.gov Automated answering system: (800) 424-5454 or (202) 512-7470
Congressional Relations	Katherine Siggerud, Managing Director, siggerudk@gao.gov, (202) 512-4400, U.S. Government Accountability Office, 441 G Street NW, Room 7125, Washington, DC 20548
Public Affairs	Chuck Young, Managing Director, youngc1@gao.gov, (202) 512-4800 U.S. Government Accountability Office, 441 G Street NW, Room 7149 Washington, DC 20548

Please Print on Recycled Paper.